IN THE
Stillness
IS THE
Dancing

MARK LINK, S.J.

by **ARGUS COMMUNICATIONS**

7440 North Natchez Avenue • Niles, Illinois 60648

International Standard Book Number: 0-913592-06-4

Contents

ACKNOWLEDGMENTS

From *Growth Games*, copyright © 1970 by Howard R. Lewis and Harold S. Streitfeld. Reprinted by permission of Harcourt Brace Jovanovich, Inc.

Media & Methods for "Automan" by Jeffrey Schrank.

"But Where?" from *Culture and Commitment: A Study of the Generation Gap* by Margaret Mead, Copyright © 1970 by Margaret Mead. Reprinted by permission of Doubleday & Company, Inc.

Reprinted with permission from *Tune In*, ed. Herman C. Ahrens, Jr. Copyright © 1968 by United Church Press.

Galaxy Music Corporation for *Nothing Fixed or Final* by Sydney Carter.

From *Seen Through Our Eyes*, edited by Michael Gecan. Copyright © 1971, 1972 by Michael Gecan. Reprinted by permission of Random House, Inc.

Look Magazine, Cowles Communications Inc., for "A Vision of the Human Revolution" by William Hedgepeth.

Excerpt from "Mini-Maxims for my Godson", by Arthur Gordon, *The Reader's Digest,* August, 1969. Copyright 1969 by The Reader's Digest Assn., Inc.

From *The Farther Reaches of Human Nature* by Abraham H. Maslow. Copyright © 1971 by Bertha G. Maslow. All rights reserved. Reprinted by permission of The Viking Press, Inc.

From *Witness*, by Whittaker Chambers. Copyright 1952 by Whittaker Chambers. Reprinted by permission of Random House, Inc.

From *Conversations with Eugene Ionesco* by Claude Bonnefoy. Translated by Jan Dawson. Copyright © 1970 by Faber and Faber Limited. Reprinted by permission of Holt, Rinehart and Winston, Inc.

Excerpt from "The Best Advice I've Ever Had" by Andre Kostelanetz, *The Reader's Digest*, March, 1957. Copyright 1957 by The Reader's Digest Assn., Inc.

Thomas Merton, *The Way of Chuang Tzu*. Copyright © 1965 by The Abbey of Gethsemani. Reprinted by permission of New Direction Publishing Corporation.

Mind Over Drugs reprinted by permission from *Time*, The Weekly Newsmagazine; © Time Inc. 1971.

Hutchinson Publishers for *Foundations of Tibetan Mysticism* by Lama Anagarika Govinda.

Modern Living reprinted by permission from *Time*, The Weekly Newsmagazine; © Time Inc. 1970.

From "*Playboy* Interview: Allen Ginsberg" *Playboy Magazine* (April 1969); copyright © 1969 by Playboy. Used with permission.

Doubleday & Company, Inc. for *The Story of My Life* by Helen Keller.

Atlantic Monthly for "Three Days to See" by Helen Keller.

Walking on Air reprinted by permission from *Time*, The Weekly Newsmagazine; © Time Inc. 1961.

Excerpt from "Hurray! It's Raining" by Elizabeth Starr Hill, *The Reader's Digest*, April, 1967. Copyright 1967 by The Reader's Digest Assn., Inc.

Fleming H. Revell Company for *Man Does Not Stand Alone* by A. Cressy Morrison.

From *To a Dancing God* by Sam Keen:
From prose abridged on pp. 117-119
From prose abridged on pp. 124
From (abridged) pp. 28-29
Copyright © 1970 by Sam Keen.

Harvard University Press for *The Feast of Fools* by Harvey Cox. Copyright © 1969 by Harvey Cox.

Herder & Herder Inc. for *Man At Play* by Hugo Rahner.

The Sign for "Celebration: What's It All About" by John F. O'Grady.

From prose abridged on p. 35 in *Apology For Wonder* by Sam Keen. Copyright © 1969 by Sam Keen.

From prose abridged, on p. 78 in *The Divine Milieu* by Pierre Teilhard de Chardin, translated by Bernard Wall. Copyright 1957 by Editions de Seuil, Paris. English translation—Copyright © 1960 by Wm. Collins Sons & Co. Ltd., London and Harper & Row, Publishers, Inc., New York.

Random House, Inc. for *The Brothers Karamozov* by Fyodor Dostoyevsky.

Houghton Mifflin Company for *On Becoming a Person* by Carl R. Rodgers.

Word, Inc., for *The Taste of New Wine* by Keith Miller. Copyright © 1965.

From *Down These Mean Streets*, by Piri Thomas Copyright © 1967 by Piri Thomas. Reprinted by permission of Alfred A. Knopf, Inc.

Mere Christianity by C. S. Lewis. Copyright 1943, 1945, 1952 by The Macmillan Company.

Ethics by Dietrich Bonhoeffer. Copyright © 1955 by The Macmillan Company. © SCM Press, Ltd. 1955.

From prose abridged on p. 87 & 153 in *Hymn of the Universe* by Pierre Teilhard de Chardin, translated by Simon Bartholomew. Copyright © 1961 by Editions du Seuil. Copyright © 1965 in the English translation by William Collins Sons & Co. Ltd., London and Harper & Row, Publishers, Inc., New York.

Catholic World for Peter J. Fleming's review of "The Age of Aquarius: Technology & Cultural Revolution".

Oxford University Press for "God's Grandeur" by Gerard Manley Hopkins.

Worship for "Prayer and Contemporary Man" by Jane Marie Richardson.

The Way for "Progress in Prayer" by Michael Lapierre.

Man's Search for Meaning. Copyright © 1959, 1962 by Viktor Frankl. Reprinted by permission of Beacon Press.

The Intellectual Life by Antonin Sertillanges. Reprinted by permission of the Mercier Press, Cork, Ireland.

Excerpts from *Opening the Bible* published by The Liturgical Press copyright © 1970 by the trustees of the Merton Legacy Trust.

DESIGN BY GENE TARPEY

PHOTO CREDITS

Ronna Baker 76
Joe Benge 66
Carol Bales 13B, 16T, 16B, 28T, 28B, 44, 49, 53, 57, 69, 80, 101, 104, 109, *110, 111*
Richard Cross 112
Mike Deane 93
John W. Glaser 20, 36, 89B
Algirdas Grigaitis *43T, 63,* 85, 105
Robert Hollis 73
Leon Isaza, S.J. 59
Robert M. Johnson 8, *11, 14, 31, 50, 54,* 92, *115*
Gene Korba 33, *35,* 41L, 41R, *98*
Chuck Lieberman 65, 119
Sr. Mary Lucas 10, *34, 51,* 68B, *91, 95, 106, 118*
Steve Matalon 68T, 72, 82R, 113B
Bob McKendrick *6, 15,* 25, 61, *74, 75, 82L, 86, 99, 114,* 116, 117
Normand Gregoire 29
Dave Povilaitis 100
Paul Sequeira *26,* 37, *39,* 40, 56, 60, 64, 81, *83,* 108
Ken Short 12, 17, *18, 19,* 30, *43B,* 45, *46,* 48, 52, 71, *78,* 79, 84, 88, *90,* 96, 97, 103
Ed Simpson *22,* cover
Gene Tarpey 9, *23,* 42, 55

4

Introduction

1

Blinded by Vision

AUTOMATED MAN

ELECTRIC CIRCUS

Computer-run projectors
rain down . . . colors and shapes.
A flashing amoeba forms on the ceiling,
drifts downward on cigarette smoke,
engulfs you, then is gone.
You are a living screen . . .
a human sliver in a dazzling
electric kaliedoscope,
a fleck of rainbow
in a swirling technological prism.

And the sound. Overpowering . . .
Bleats. Moans. Crowd noises.
Pandemonium so amplified it is not heard
but felt.

And the mass of humanity, the rubbing bodies.
The feel of cloth and skin against your skin.
Heat and sweat and smells and closeness . . .

Overall (perhaps surprisingly)
the effect is pleasant, and you're likely
to go home feeling atingle, possibly euphoric . . .
One aim of such go-go joints
is to produce a nondrug turn-on . . .

You may indeed have a sensory awakening.
But even an Electric Circus . . .
can get boring.
For all the sensory excitement it offers,
more and greater stimuli are needed
for the same result.

Howard R. Lewis and
Harold S. Streitfeld
Growth Games

BORED?

We click on our TV set,
and the world parades through our home.
We watch what other generations
never dreamed of:
two earth men, in a rover,
traversing the chalky surface of the moon.

But minutes later,
we yawn, click off the set, and go to bed.
In less than half an hour
the "greatest achievement since creation"
no longer engages us.

Bombings, hijacked planes, and
incredible cruelties
flash before our eyes in "living color".
We respond by
lighting up another cigarette
or opening a second can of beer.
Who can feel outrage and indignation
every single telecast?
Who can help but become bored?

CYBORG

Just when we were beginning to realize
the aptness of McLuhan's suggestion
that the automobile was . . .
an extension of man,
the automobile is threatening to turn man
into an extension of itself.

Those hard shells we familiarly call cars
are more than
extensions of our feet and psyches.
They live with us. We co-inhabit.

In fact the relationship between auto and driver
is best thought of as symbiotic—
the living together of two species.
The auto-driver is a cyborg,
a half-man and half machine—
a centaur of technology.

Jeffrey Schrank
"Automan"

9

BUT WHERE?
(Shannon Dickson, 15 year-old Texan boy)

My generation is being used
almost like a machine . . .
But how shall we change? . . .

Computers take the place of minds;
electronics are taking over,
only confusing things more.

The answer is out there somewhere.

Margaret Mead
Culture and Commitment

LOOK AT ME

My mind,
Hidden now behind its hollow wall,
Cries out to you—
"Look at me!"
Look at me while I still breathe . . .

Or am I so numeralled, digited to zero,
That I no longer pass reflection?

If so,
Then, in the name of God,
Move aside and let my shadow pass
To its appointed nothingness.

J. A. Christensen
"Fiction of Loneliness"

WORLD, I AM YOUTH

World, I am Youth, unsettled and searching,
Exploring the heights and the plain.
I wander your deserts, thirsty and pale,
I weep in the beating rain.
Ascend I the mountains with eagerness,
Hungry, and seeking my goal,
Then into barbs of stinging thorns
I fall with deluded soul.
In your shadows of dusk I tremble.
I fear death and even life.
Tomorrow I laugh, and confidence
Pervades my daily strife.
World, I am Youth, the hope of your day,
I'm bewildered and young in this land.
I'm searching your paths for a vision called truth
—Give me your hand.

Anonymous

LOST!

And now, it is so early,
There's nothing I can see.
Before the world, or after?
Wherever can I

be?

Sydney Carter

WHAT ARE WE
WAITING FOR?

There are fathers
waiting until other obligations
are less demanding
to become acquainted with their sons . . .
There are mothers who . . .
sincerely intend to be more attentive
to their daughters . . .
There are husbands and wives
who are going to be more understanding . . .
But time does not draw people closer . . .

[W]hen in the world
are we going to begin to live
as if we understood that this is life?
This is our time, our day . . .
and it is passing.
What are we waiting for?

Richard L. Evans

LIFE: quantity or quality?

"I'm going to transfer out of this school,"
said a college student.
"I'm so busy cramming for tests,
I haven't time to learn.
I've almost forgotten
how to sit back and really appreciate
a good book."

Is this true of us, also?
Are we so busy with life
that we haven't time to live?
Have we, perhaps, forgotten
how to sit back and really appreciate life?

What does it profit a man
if he is so busy with the quantity of life
that he loses its quality?

LIFE OR DEATH

He who isn't busy being born
is busy dying.

Bob Dylan

DEAUTOMATIZATION: gear down

Perhaps, we need to undergo a process
which some call "deautomatization".
Don't we tend to become
somewhat automated and programmed?
We tend to perceive and respond to things
in a habitual way—almost mechanical.

Pausing to reflect shakes up this fixed way
of perceiving and responding to life and people.
It exorcises the automated "demon" within us.
It exposes us
to an entirely new way of looking at things.
It liberates us from
our programmed, automated existence;
it invites us to explore reality with new eyes
and a new mind.

I SAW WAS WAS SAW

I remember one day
when we were all reading aloud
from the same book.
I saw the word "was",
and the thought flashed through my mind
that if you spelled "was" backwards,
you got "saw".
At that time it was an exciting discovery,
and I raised my hand
and told the class what I had noticed.

Mary Wilke
in *Seen Through Our Eyes*

Two men looked out through prison bars,
One saw mud; the other stars.

Oscar Wilde
"Reading Gaol"

The way we look at life
often spells the difference between
excitement and boredom,
beauty and ugliness,
apathy and creativity.

WHO CHANGED?

A distraught woman in a Boston hotel . . .
called the manager:
"I am dizzy and faint, my whole body is trembling.
Somebody in the next room
has been banging a piano the whole day.
If you don't have it stopped at once I shall collapse,
and you will be responsible."

"I wish I could help you madam,"
the hotel manager replied,
"but I don't dare. That pianist is rehearsing for
his concert tonight in Symphony Hall—it's Paderewski."

"Really!" quavered the complainant.
"Oh, that's different!"

Immediately she began inviting friends
to come over and listen with her.

Fulton Oursler
"The Way You Look At It"

NOW IS . . .

This moment is all that exists.
This fleeting instant—this now—
is the only reality.
The past is gone forever.
The future is not yet born . . .

You can physically *see* and hear
only what *is* at this moment.
You can have sensory awakening
only if you experience the now.

If you bring your mind from miles away
to the activity of the moment . . .
you gradually experience
a surprising sense of well-being.

Indeed, tuning into the now
is one gateway
to perceiving eternity . . .
Time is defined as the interval
between two events.
When you are in the now;
there is no interval.
Only the event alone.

Howard R. Lewis and
Harold S. Streitfeld
Growth Games

GRASP THE REAL

Do and dare what is right,
not swayed by the whim of the moment.
Bravely take hold of the real,
not dallying now with what might be.

Deitrich Bonhoeffer
The Way To Freedom

MY FAULT

Nothing can work me damage except
myself;
I am a real sufferer by my fault.

St. Bernard

TIME TO GO, TO RUN . . .

Up, quick, if you can.
It's long past time to go.
You've stayed so long
you've lost yourself
and now exist cut off from
all of you that's human.
You're civilized beyond your senses:
out of touch, narcotized,
mechanized, Westernized,
with bleached-out eyes
that yearn for natural light . . .
The Good Life,
so devoutly sought,

has grown blind, bland,
banal and numb . . .
It's time to go, to run,
to rise up,
fling open the window,
thaw the blood, prance high
in the wet grass—
to shout and feel and seek
new rootholds in the nourishing earth.
Rise up now beyond your head.
Short-circuit civilization. ←

William Hedgepeth
"A Vision of the Human Revolution"

UNBUTTON
YOUR RAINCOAT

. . . when I was a Boy Scout,
I had a troop leader who . . . would take us
on hikes not saying a word,
and then challenge us to describe
what we had observed: trees, plants,
birds, wildlife, everything.

Invariably we hadn't seen
a quarter as much as he had,
nor half enough to satisfy him.
"Creation is all around you," he would cry,
waving his arms in vast inclusive circles.
"But you're keeping it out . . .
Stop wearing your raincoat in the shower!"

I've never forgotten the ludicrous image
of a person standing in a shower bath
with a raincoat buttoned up to his chin.
It was a memorable exhortation
to heightened awareness.

The best way to discard the raincoat, I've found,
is to expose yourself to new experiences.
It's routine that dulls the eye and deadens the ear . . .
Get rid of that raincoat and let creation in!

Arthur Gordon
"Mini-Maxims
for My Godson"

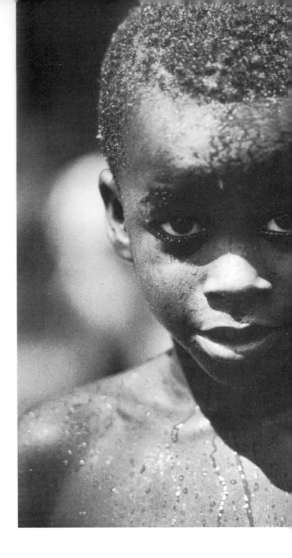

COSMIC CIRCUS

The night was nearly still,
and an inky black
covered the woods and water.
It was so quiet that I could hear
the back-and-forth calls of gulls
and smell the lingering scent
of the day's catch.
I heard the gentle swash
of the sea against the sturdy dock.

As I leaned back I saw
patterns of constellations stand out
in bas relief from the darkness.

16

STEP SOFTLY

Step softly under snow or rain
To find the place where men can pray;
The way is all so very plain
That we may lose the way.

Gilbert K. Chesterton

Happiness grows at our own firesides,
and is not
to be picked in strangers' gardens.

Douglas Jerrold

AMAZING GRACE

Holding a twig in one's hand,
or a flower,
one finds oneself absorbed
in its singularity,
in its own inexhaustibility . . .
its own utter distinctness . . .

Suddenly the world
seems overridingly mysterious.
Dimensions beyond dimensions
are revealed in it.
Nothing is too simple,
too ordinary, too routine,
to escape one's wonderment.

Michael Novak

I saw a shooting star
glide across the heavens in an arch.
The lights of the stars blinked
as they followed preset patterns—
infinitely complex, remarkably organized.
It was hard for me to realize
on this calm night in this cozy setting
that each of those friendly stars
was a sun, and each sun just
one small part of thousands of galaxies,
and all this grandeur was not nearly all
that there was,
but only that small part
that I could see.

WONDER FUND

The world
will never starve for wonders;
but only
for the want of wonder.

Gilbert K. Chesterton

FRESH AND EXCITING

There is only one way to attend
a circus or visit a zoo,
and that is with a little child.
Before long you find yourself entering
the world of wonder
that lies fresh and exciting
within each child.
If you're wise, you'll
let the child be your guide.

Watch a child in a park or a woods,
and you'll be amazed at how quickly
he discovers what we have lost:
a world of "flutterbys" and "grasschoppers".
He "sees" a world we only look at;
he "listens" to sounds we only hear.

"Unless you change
and become like children,
you will never enter
the kingdom of heaven."

Matthew 18:3

SURE SIGN

The search
for the exotic, the strange, the unusual . . .
has often taken the form of pilgrimages,
of turning away from the world,
the "Journey to the East",
to another country
or to a different Religion.

The great lesson
from true mystics, from the Zen monks,
and now also from . . . psychologists—

18

LOOKING DEEPLY

For many years,
I was the self-appointed inspector
of snowstorms and rainstorms
and I did my duty faithfully.

Henry David Thoreau

MENAGERIE OF WONDER

Rody is growing no end.
You have to laugh to see the whole crew
cutting out Christmas cookies.

Rody would clap her hands and
squeal with delight
every time she got a half-way decent one.

We got quite a menagerie
of odd-looking animals and bells and
stars—but they still taste good.

Had to laugh at Rody when she was
licking the pan.
She said in all seriousness,
"You know, Mommy,
this is a good place to live."

Rosemary Schmit
Letter to the author

FOR ONE WHO CAN SEE . . .

The greatest thing a human soul
ever does in this world is to see something
and tell what it saw in a plain way.

Hundreds of people can talk
for one who can think,
and thousands can think
for one who can see.

To see clearly is poetry, prophecy
and religion—all in one.

John Ruskin

that the sacred is *in* the ordinary . . .
and that
travel may be flight from confronting the sacred—
this lesson can be easily lost.

To be looking elsewhere
for miracles
is to me a sure sign of the ignorance
that everything is miraculous.

A. H. Maslow
The Farther Reaches of Human Nature

SACRED

Nothing here below is profane
for those who know how to see.

On the contrary,
everything is sacred.

Teilhard de Chardin

LIVING WONDER

The farm was your kingdom,
and the world lay far beyond the
protecting walls
thrown up by work and love.

It is true that comic strips
were not encouraged,
comic books were banned,
the radio could be turned on
only by permission
which was seldom given (or asked),
and you saw few movies.

But you grew in the presence of the
eternal wonders . . .
Thus, as children, you experienced
two of the most important things
men ever know—
the wonder of life and
the wonder of the universe,
the wonder of life within
the wonder of the universe.

More important,
you knew them not from books,
not from lectures,
but simply from living among them.

Most important,
you knew them with reverence and awe—
that reverence and awe
that has died out of the modern world and
been replaced by man's monkey-like amazement
at the cleverness of his inventive brain.

Whittaker Chambers
Witness

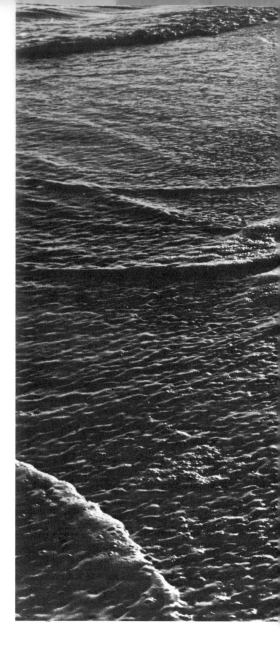

UNANSWERED

For his epitaph
a Frenchman chose these words.
"Here lies a man
who went out of the world
without knowing
why he came into it."

Maurice Sheehy
Head Over Heels

SPHERES OF SILENCE

Silence helps one enter
into more elevated spheres
and listen to
the mysterious voice of God.

Pius XII

ONLY IN LONELINESS

A man must get away
now and then
to experience loneliness.
Only those who learn how to live
in loneliness
can come to know themselves
and life.

I go out there and walk
and look at the trees and sky.
I listen to the sounds of loneliness.
I sit on a rock or stump
and say to myself,

"Who are you, Sandburg?
Where have you been,
and where are you going?"

Carl Sandburg

✓ FIRST STEP

As you sit in silence
on a lonely beach
or a drifting sand dune,
you discover the possibilities
for a new world
and a new self.

You may not be transformed
by the experience.
But if it stirs within you
the desire to be—
then you've taken the first step.

CROWD SHROUD

Life has to be thoroughly impregnated with solitude in order to be liveable. Everyone needs a personal space to live in . . . [M]y characters are simply people who don't know how to be alone . . . That's why in certain of my plays, the characters are always with one another and always chattering. They are noisy because they have forgotten the meaning and value of solitude. And this is why they are alone—alone in a quite different way. There is a noise in a *Stroll in the Air* too, people talking, saying any old thing be-cause they are cut off, separated from themselves and therefore from other people . . . Look at crowds, they're depersonalized, people don't have "faces" in a crowd . . . or if they have a face, it's a collective face, and monstrous. It is the face of anger, of destruction, the face of hell. Everyone has the same face in a crowd, whether it is uniform or formless.

Eugene Ionesco
Conversations with Eugene Ionesco

GET NEXT TO YOURSELF

I recommend strongly that every executive
set aside a little time . . . to decide

where he is going,
what are his priorities,
what are his ambitions.
Do you know whether you are going
in the right direction,
and most of all,
where do you want to get?

Dr. William G. Menninger

UNDERSTATEMENT

I cannot overstate the importance
of the habit of quiet meditation
for health of body, mind and spirit.

Dr. W. R. Luxton

FIND THE ARTICHOKES

When I arrived at Matisse's home . . .
I was not only late but exhausted.
The exuberant artist listened good-humoredly . . .
"My friend, you must find
the artichokes in your life!"

I was frankly baffled . . .
Then Matisse, motioning . . . to follow him,
stepped outside.
We walked through the garden until
we came to the artichokes.

"Every morning,
after having worked for a stretch,
I come here," he said,
"and watch the play of light and shade
on the leaves.
Though I have painted over 2000 canvases,
I always find here new combinations of
colors and fantastic patterns.
No one is allowed to disturb me in this
ritual of discovery;
it gives me fresh inspiration, necessary relaxation
and a new perspective toward my work!"

This struck me forcefully,
for Matisse was telling me gently that every day
should have its moments of silence and contemplation.
He was saying that thoughts may wither
and actions go stale if we are not wise enough
to pause now and then to restore
the mental and psychic fuel
burned in the course of the day.

Andre Kostelanetz
"The Best Advice I've Ever Had"

DRAGON POWER

The wise man, when he must govern,
knows how to do nothing.
Letting things alone,
he rests in his original nature.
If he loves his own person enough
to let it rest in its original truth,
he will govern others without hurting them.
Let him keep the deep drives in his own guts
from going into action.

Let him keep still,
not looking, not hearing.
Let him sit like a corpse,
with the dragon power alive all around him.
In complete silence,
his voice will be like thunder.
His movements will be invisible,
like those of a spirit,
but the powers of heaven will go with them.

Chuang-tzu

ESCAPE "ESCAPE"

Harvard researchers have confirmed . . .
that actual physiological changes
sometimes occur during meditation . . .

Meditation, the researchers suggest,
may even be of value
in alleviating such problems as
alcoholism and drug addiction.

Time magazine

SLOW ME DOWN, LORD

Give me, amid the confusion of the day,
the calmness of the everlasting hills.
Break the tensions
of my nerves and muscles with the soothing music
of the singing streams that live in my memory.
Help me to know the magical,
restoring power of sleep.
Teach me the art of taking minute vacations—
of slowing down to look at a flower,
to chat with a friend, to pat a dog,
to read a few lines from a good book.

Remind me each day
of the fable of the hare and the tortoise,
that I may know
that the race is not always to the swift—
there is more to life than increasing its speed.
Let me look upward
into the branches of the towering oak and know
that it grew great and strong
because it grew slowly and well.

Slow me down, Lord, and inspire me to send
my roots deep in to the soil of life's enduring values
that I may grow toward the stars
of my greater destiny.

Richard Cardinal Cushing

2

Give Me Madness

LIBERATION

SET THE MOOD

A first step in effective meditation
is creating a mood
of concentration and repose.
One way to achieve this is
by focusing on one's breathing.

Breathing has been described as the
"vehicle of spiritual experience,
the mediator between body and mind . . .

"It is the first step
towards the transformation of the body
from a more or less
passively and unconsiously functioning
physical organ
into a . . . tool of a
perfectly developed and enlightened mind."

Lama Govinda
Foundations of Tibetan Mysticism

DEEPEN IT

Make yourself completely comfortable.
Lie down on your back,
if you wish.

II

Observe your breathing.
Don't change or alter it;
just observe it.

Are you breathing smoothly,
rhythmically?
Or is it jerky and uneven?
Without strain, try to even it out.

How deeply are you breathing?
Is it shallow?
Gently, try to deepen it.

Is your breathing rapid?
Gently, try to slow it down.

For the next four or five minutes,
close your eyes
and try to establish a pattern
of slow, deep, even breathing.

FANTASY FLIGHT — TO REALITY

Assume a comfortable position.
Relax completely.
Set up a pattern of smooth breathing.

II

As you inhale, imagine
streams of energy entering your body,
rushing through all the pores of your skin:
Picture this energy
in the form of light.

At the height of your inhalation
imagine your whole body glowing
with light and tingling with strength.

As you exhale, imagine this light
streaming out of your body
through the fingers of your hands
and the toes of your feet —
leaving your entire body invigorated,
strengthened and relaxed.

Continue this exercise for the next
four or five minutes — or as long
as you wish.

SOUND SEARCH

There are mechanical sounds:
the click-clack of a ping-pong ball,
the humming of a neon light bulb,
the wail of a siren at midnight.

There are nature sounds:
the coo of pigeons in the park,
the pinging of rain or sleet on a window pane,
the swishing of wind in tall trees.

There are human sounds:
the roar of a crowd at a ball game,
voices in the dark,
the gasping of an old man in a hospital ward.
There is the voice of the one you love most.

II

How do these various sounds make you feel?
If you suddenly lost your hearing,
what sounds would you miss most?

WHITE NOISE

With noise pollution
under attack across the U.S.,
it hardly seems a propitious time
to produce noisemakers.
But a few manufacturers are doing just that . . .

The most widely used of the noisemakers
produce a mild form of radio static
called "white noise" by engineers.
Turned down to a discreet volume,
the static
masks distracting outside noises and
disturbing interior echoes. . .

For those who cannot sleep
amid too much quiet . . .
Syntonic Research has produced a simple record
with one side devoted entirely to
the sound of surf,
and the other to tropical bird noises.

Time magazine

II

For the next few minutes,
listen to the sounds around you.
Try to identify what they are and
where they come from.

Recall the sounds you heard.
Which sound stands out in your memory? Why?
Did you hear sounds that you were unaware of
previously?

MUSIC MASSAGE

A drum and bugle corps,
making Main Street echo with
brass and thunder;
a young mother, humming to
her sleepy-eyed baby;
a concert pianist,
filling Carnegie Hall with music;
a boy, crooning in a shower;
marchers, singing
"We Shall Overcome";
a rock group, counter-pointing
to strobe lights —
music has a mystery that
soothes, exalts, transforms.

II

Put on a long-play record or
a cassette tape of music.
Make yourself completely comfortable.

Concentrate on the music, and
consciously try to follow the instruments,
the melody, and the total movement
of the piece.

Let the music penetrate your whole body
and bounce around inside you.
Let it awaken your emotions.
Let it move your body.

BY GOSH, IT'S GOOD

O body swayed to music,
    O brightening glance.
How can we know
    the dancer from the dance?

William Butler Yeats

Music, rhythm and dancing
are excellent ways of moving toward
the discovering of identity.
We are built in such a fashion that
this kind of trigger,
this kind of stimulation,
tends to do all kinds of things
to our . . . feelings and to our emotions . . .

In experientially empty people . . .
people who do not know
what is going on inside themselves
and who live by clocks, schedules, rules . . .
this is a way of discovering
what the self is like.

There are signals from inside,
there are voices that yell out,
"By gosh this is good, don't ever doubt it!"
This is the path, one of the ways
that we try to teach self-actualization
and the discovery of self.
This discovery of identity comes
via the impulse voices,
via the ability to listen to your own guts,
and to their reactions
and to what is going on inside of you.

A. H. Maslow
The Farther Reaches of Human Nature

OWWOOOHMMM

I began to feel
a funny tingling in my feet that spread until
my whole body was one rigid electric tingling—
a solid mass of lights.
It was around 8 P.M. now
and I'd been facing the John Hancock Building,
which was beginning to light up.
I felt like the building, except that it wasn't alive
and I was.
Then I felt a rigidity inside my body,
almost like a muscle armor plating.
With all this electric going up and down
and this rigid muscle thing,
I had to straighten my back to make a clear passage
for whatever flow there was;

Suddenly, I realized I was going through
some kind of weird trance thing
like I'd read about in books.
But it wasn't mystical.
It was the product of six continuous hours of
chanting *Om*, regularizing breathing and
altering rhythmic body chemistry.

Allen Ginsberg
Playboy

II

"Om" is regarded in India as the greatest mantra,
representing God in his fullness.

It is used in non-Buddhist meditation,
not for its sacred symbolism
but for the vibrations induced by chanting it.
If continued long enough, the effect is like
an internal massage, heightened when you
experience it in a meditative state.

Om can be divided equally into
three prolonged syllables, covering a range of sound
For the first part of an exhalation
make the sound "owww" as in "cow".
Glide into "oooh" as in "chew".
Conclude with the final syllable "mmmm",
until you run out of breath.
Inhale and resume.

Howard R. Lewis and
Harold S. Streifeld
Growth Games

KOAN: PRISON BREAK

Koan (pronounced ko-an) is a Japanese word
for a problem or riddle
that cannot be solved by reasoning,
but only by the awakening of something
at a level deeper than the mind.

The purpose of a koan is to help a person
to break out of the prison of the mind
to discover, not what is thought,
but what really is.

One of the classic koans is this:
what is the sound of one hand clapping?
Another is this:
without speaking and without silence,
how do you express truth?

FLY FREELY

Try "playing spectator"
to your own thoughts.

"Chaudhuri, drawing on yoga,
explains the method this way.

[R]esolve to do nothing, to think nothing . . .
relax completely and let go . . .
stepping out of the stream of
ever-changing ideas and feelings
which your mind is . . .

Refuse to be submerged in the current.
Changing the metaphor, it may be said,
watch your ideas, feelings and wishes
fly across the mental firmament
like a flock of birds.
Let them fly freely.
Just keep watch.
Don't allow the birds
to carry you off into the clouds."

Edward Maupin
"Meditation"
in *Ways of Growth*

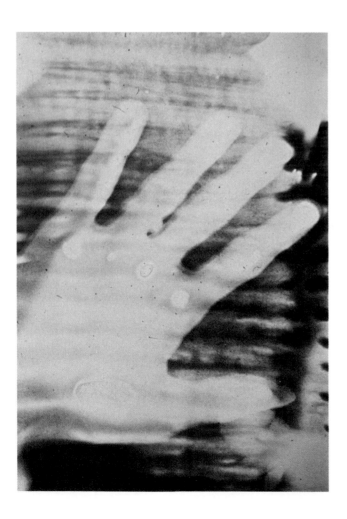

34

HANDS WITH SUNBEAMS

The hands of those I meet
are dumbly eloquent to me.
The touch of some hands is an impertinence.
I have met people so empty of joy,
that when I clasped their frosty finger-tips,
it seemed as if I were shaking hands with
a northeast storm.

Others there are whose hands have sunbeams in them,
so that their grasp warms my heart.
It may be only the clinging touch of a child's hand;
but there is as much potential for sunshine in it for me
as there is in a loving glance for others.

Helen Keller
The Story of My Life

II

Feel the beat of your heart,
the passage of breath through your nostrils,
the sturdy support of a chair against your back,
the grip of shoes on your feet,
the clinging of clothes around your body,
the coolness or warmth of air immersing you.

III

Touch can thrill the heart and exalt the spirit.
It is the poetry of silence.
Between two people,
touch can be more eloquent than speech,
more reaffirming than words.

DON'T MISS THE MIRACLE

I, who cannot see, find hundreds of things
to interest me through mere touch.
I feel the delicate symmetry of a leaf.
I pass my hands lovingly
about the smooth skin of a silver birch,
or the rough shaggy bark of a pine . . .

I feel the delightful, velvety texture of a flower,
and discover its remarkable convolutions;
and something of the miracle of Nature
is revealed to me.
Occasionally, if I am very fortunate,
I place my hand gently on a small tree and feel
the happy quiver of a bird in full song . . .

At times my heart cries out with longing
to see these things.
If I can get so much pleasure from mere touch,
how much more beauty must be revealed
by sight.
Yet, those who have eyes apparently see little.
The panorama of color and action
which fills the world is taken for granted . . .
It is . . . a great pity that, in the world of light,
the gift of sight
is used only as a mere convenience rather than
as a means of adding fullness to life.

Helen Keller
"Three Days To See"

II

Try focusing on some object, as though
you saw it for the first time.
Take a tree, for example.
Study its shape, texture, colors.
Ponder its sun-searching branches,
its delicate leaves, that drink in life from the sun
and pass it on to the atmosphere which you breathe.

Think about its life-giving cluster of roots,
combing the soil for mineral food.
Why did *this* tree come to be? Why any tree?

E-MOTION

At the end of the narrow dirt runway,
the pencil-thin Negro
poises disjointedly, like a puppet
whose strings are loose.

Then he prances forward,
flapping his skinny arms
and kicking his knees almost to his chest.
Suddenly, his left foot
slams savagely into the take-off board.
His eyes bug, his face contorts,
and his legs pedal furiously
as he springs into trajectory.
His left hand claws upward through the air
as though searching for something.

Time magazine

II

Study a moving object:
a person walking down the street,
a flower bobbing on the end of a stem,
the sweep of the second hand
on your watch.

What does the motion remind you of?
How would you describe the feeling
it gives you?

RSVP

What is this life,
if full of care,
We have no time
to stand and stare?

William Henry Davies

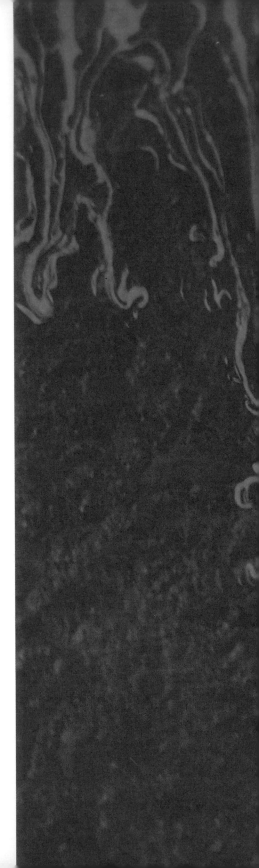

CONCERTS IN COLOR

Color is king these days.
Skirts explode in sunrise orange
and peppermint stripes.
Pants sprout in green and
bloom in gold.

Telephones purr in purple
and vibrate in red.
Cars cruise in coupled-color
and chrome;
bucket seats growl in
black and yellow tiger skin.

It's a color world we live and cry in.
Red can symbolize courage or action,
but also hate and carnage.
Purple can speak of heroism
and royalty; it can also signal
passion and mystery.
Yellow says cowardice and sickness,
but also echoes cheeriness and wealth.
Green symbolizes envy,
but it also speaks of spring and freshness.

What makes color speak to people
in different ways in varied situations?

II

Focus on a color.
Think of one word that describes
how this color makes you feel.

Now let your eyes take in a combination
of colors to blend with your color.
What feeling does this "harmony"
give you?

Imagine that you will never see again.
What sight will you miss most?

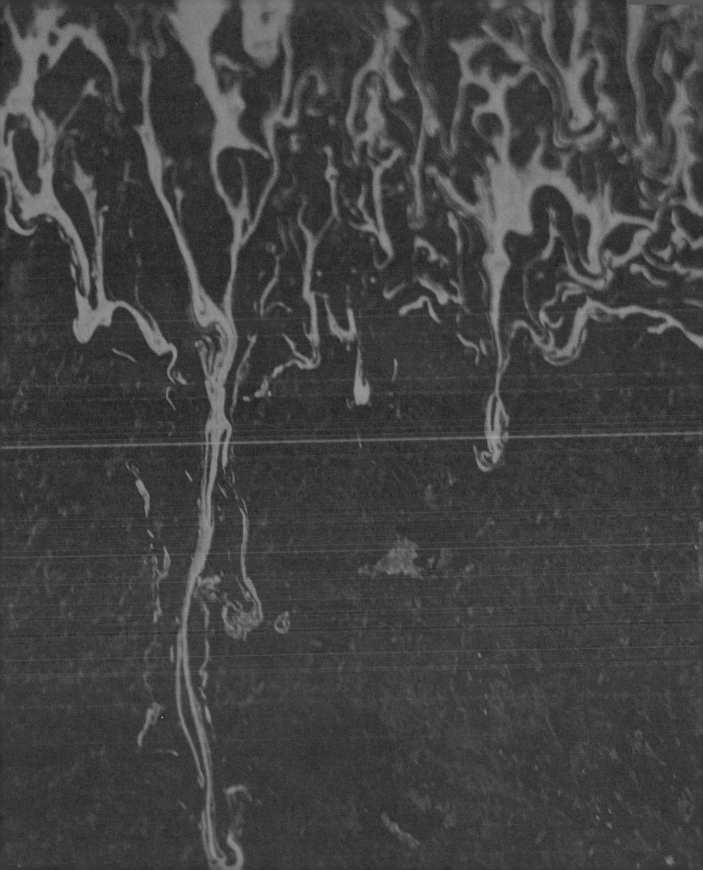

"HURRAY! IT'S RAINING"

We had spent several weeks in southern Spain,
at the hottest time of the year.
Early every morning my young son
went to the balcony of our hotel
to see what kind of day it would be,
and every day it was the same—
inexhaustibly sunny—
until one morning I heard a whoop of joy
and the exaultant words,
"Hurray! It's raining!"

Glorious to see the dusty streets and rooftops
running with rain!

Delightful to breathe the cleansed air,
to smell the wet earth!

Through the whole of that streaming day,
Longfellow's poem sang in my mind:

How beautiful is the rain!
After the dust and heat,
In the broad and fiery street,
In the narrow lane,
How beautiful is the rain!

Elizabeth Starr Hill
"Hurray! It's Raining!"

II

Imagine lying on the hot sand of a beach
that has absorbed the torrid heat
of a full day's sun.
Suddenly, a cloud, a cool breeze, and
gentle drops of rain.

Imagine the raindrops falling on the lake,
forming tiny little ringlets
that appear and disappear.

Listen to the rain falling on the lake,
on the beach around you, on leaves of
nearby trees, on metal objects close to or
on the beach.

Can you feel the soothing rain, massaging
your body, running down your arms, your legs,
your face, your shoulders?
Marvel at its long journey from the clouds to you.

Taste the rain, as it falls on your parched lips
and trickles across them.

Feel and smell the freshness of the air,
washed clean by the rain.

Just lie quiet for a while, enjoying the full sensation
of the rain.

YOUR HEART

When you sleep or
are knocked unconscious, it keeps going.
When you run, it runs faster.
If you should starve,
it would be the last part of your body
to yield up its tissue.

Each day it pumps enough blood
through 60,000 miles
of veins and capillaries
to fill a 4,000 gallon tank—
and it never stops for a rest.

Man's heart is almost as much a mystery
as is his brain.
"The heart has reasons the mind
knows not of," says the poet.
Tender-hearted, light-hearted,
good-hearted, lion-hearted—
they are more than idle phrases.
They say something about the mystery
of you—and your heart.

II

Feel your heart beat.
Put your hand on your pulse
and be sensitive to its rhythm.

How does it keep going?
How did it start?
What makes it keep beating,
even in sleep, or
when I am knocked unconscious?

How many beats has it made
since it started?
How many has it left,
before it stops?

LIFE, THE SCULPTOR

Life is a sculptor and shapes all living things;
an artist that designs every leaf of every tree,
that colours the flowers, the apple, the forest,
and the plumage of the bird of paradise . . .

Life is a musician and has taught each bird
to sing its love songs,
the insects to call each other
in the music of their multitudinous sounds . . .

Life is a chemist that gives taste
to our fruits and spices
and perfume to the rose.
Life synthesizes new substances
which Nature has not yet provided
to balance its processes
and to destroy invading life.

A. Cressy Morrison
Man Does Not Stand Alone

II

Think about your life.
How did it begin; how does it continue?
Where is it headed?

NOTHING DISAPPEARS

Science . . . tells us that nothing in nature,
not even the tiniest particle, can disappear
without a trace.
Nature does not know extinction.
All it knows is transformation . . .

And everything science has taught me . . .
strengthens my belief in the continuity of
our spiritual existence after death.
Nothing disappears without a trace.

Wernher von Braun
This Week magazine

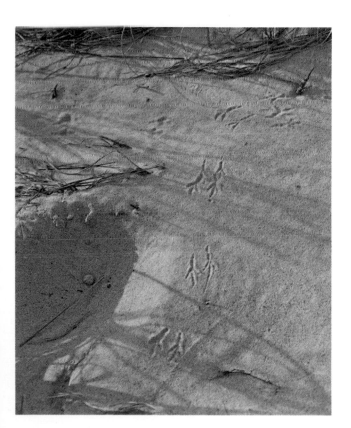

LIFE CYCLES

Biologically speaking,
the large number of cell events
which occur in childhood
gives the child an instinctive impression
of long time,
whereas owing to the slower action
of the cells in age,
it would seem that time passes very swiftly.

Life cycles may seem to have no relation
to absolute time which we measure by the movements
of the heavenly bodies . . .

It is possible that the scientists are right,
and that we, of we attain immortality,
will measure time by events,
and not by astronomy?

A. Cressy Morrison
Man Does Not Stand Alone

II

Did you ever listen to your watch ticking?
What is it saying?
Can you feel time?
Put your hand to your heart,
to the "organic clock" within you.
Feel its rhythm? What does it say?

ACTION OR ATROPHY

Monet was painting great pictures at 86.
Titian put the last brush stroke to the
"Battle of Lepanto" at 98;
he finished his "Last Supper" at 99.

Goethe finished "Faust" at 81.
Tennyson wrote "Crossing the Bar"
when he was 83.
Voltaire was still penning plays when he
died at the age of 84.

Wagner wrote his finest operas in the
final years of his life, "Parsifal" in the last year.
He died at the age of 70.

At 74 Verdi composed his "Othello";
at 80 he produced his famous "Falstaff".

"At 50 the mind hasn't yet reached its zenith.
At 60 it is at its best and from then on
declines so gradually that at 80 those who have
kept themselves mentally alert
can be just as productive as at 30.
Memory may slip a bit,
but judgment and reason may actually improve,
and creative imagination is scarcely touched by age . . ."

Marie Beynon Ray

Only the very exceptional push these resources
to their extremes of use . . .
Men habitually use only a small part of
the powers which they actually possess.

William James

GIVE ME MADNESS

God, I want to surrender
"to the rhythm of music and sea,
to the seasons of ebb and flow,
to the tidal surge of love.

I am tired of being hard,
tight, controlled,
tensed against tenderness,
afraid of softness.
I am tired of directing my world,
making, doing, shaping.

Tension is ecstasy in chains.
The muscles are tightened to prevent trembling.
Nerves strain to prevent trust,
hope, relaxation . . .

Surrender is a risk no sane man may take.
Sanity never surrendered
is a burden no man may carry.

God, give me madness
that does not destroy
wisdom,
responsibility,
love."

Sam Keen
To A Dancing God

3

Fantasy to Stillness

CELEBRATION

DREAM

In flights of wild fantasy,
I've streaked across the sky,
tunnelled the clouds and touched
the stars.

In daring ecstasy,
I've fled my craft,
walked on the wind and
painted rainbows.

I've stowed away on meteors,
trespassed the Milky Way—
planted my own flag
on the moon.

I've talked with eagles
and followed the flights of birds
to worlds
you've never dreamed of.

Laughing in symphony with
thunder, and
playing tag with lightening bolts,
I've kicked my shoes and gone unshod—
leaped out of my skin,
and played
with God.

II

Imagine yourself flying above the earth
in an open aircraft—better yet, like a
bird—free to soar and swoop, glide and turn.

Dive riotously through a layer of clouds,
and burst into song at the sight of the hills,
carpeted in green and patterned with flowers.

Then, soar, again, up beyond the fleecy white
into the high blue—and rest, coasting in the
warmth of the sun.

THOUGH TRUMPETS SOUND

O fantasy, that at times
   does so snatch us out of
Ourselves that we are conscious
   of naught, even
Though a thousand trumpets sound about us,
Who makes these, if the senses
   set naught before thee?

Dante
The Divine Comedy

FANTASY FLIGHT

Assume a comfortable position.
Relax any part of your body
that seems to be tense.

When you are ready, mentally,
that is *in your imagination*,
get up and leave this room.
Go to any place of your choice.
There is only one stipulation:
no one may accompany you or be with you there.

Where are you?
What objects do you see?
Pick out three of the objects and study them carefully.
Touch them, if you wish. Do so lovingly and gently.

If you had to dispose of all but one of these objects,
which would you keep? Dispose of all but that one.

Now listen carefully. What sounds do you hear?
Let yourself be bathed by these sounds.
Now dispose with all but one of these sounds.
Which did you keep?

Now, imagine that you could invite one person
to be with you in this place.
Who would you choose? Why?

If you could choose just one topic to talk about
with that person, what would you choose?

INTO THE BEYOND

I hear beyond the range of sound,
    I see beyond the range of sight
New earths and skies and seas abound,
    And in my day the sun doth pale his light.

Henry Thoreau

WHAT IS "REALLY REAL"?

Fantasy is the richest source of human creativity.
Theologically speaking,
it is the image of the creator God in man . . .

In many cultures
fantasy has been carefully nurtured . . .
In ours, we have ignored fantasy, depreciated it,
or tried to pretend it wasn't really there.
After all, *we* are "realists". . .

We have drawn a line between fact and fantasy,
and allowed the term "reality"
to be used only for the former . . .

Today, however, there are indications
that we may be ready
not only to reinstate fantasy,
but perhaps even to begin defining reality
so that fantasy is not left completely out . . .
Historians of science
now assign more importance
than they once did
to hunches, insights, and creative flashes.
They insist that real advances in science
come when someone leaps out
of existing paradigms
and creates a new way of envisioning things . . .

In fantasy, no holds are barred.
We suspend . . . the whole structure
of everyday "reality".
In fantasy we become
not only our ideal selves,
but totally different people.
We abolish the limits of our powers
and perceptions.
We soar.

Harvey Cox
The Feast of Fools

RIDDLE OF REALITY

The important thing is never to stop questioning.
Curiosity has its own reason for existing.
One cannot help but be in awe
when he contemplates the mysteries of eternity,
of life, of the marvelous structures of reality . . .
Never lose a holy curiosity.

Albert Einstein

It is man's destiny
to ponder on the riddle of existence and,
as a by-product of his wonderment,
to create a new life on this earth.

Charles Kettering

WELCOME MY STRANGENESS

SK: Damn it! Why did you trip me?

Rock: I didn't trip you.
I'm just lying here in my space conversing
with the sky and ground and you come and kick me.

SK: Well, never mind that.
I see now that you are just about the right shape and
size for a wall I am building.

Rock: First you accuse me of abusing you,
but now it is clear that you are . . .
the aggressor who is lacking in regard for me . . .
You still haven't seen me. All you can see is a use
to which I may be put. Why don't you
exercise your facility of wonder for a moment.

SK: I suppose I could try.
What would you like me to do?

Rock: Look at the nuances of color in me, for a beginning.
 Then you might notice the gracefulness of my form
 (far too fine to be hidden in a wall).
 Finally, if you can muster sufficient imagination . . .
 ask yourself the fantastic question of
 what my reality is like from the inside . . .

SK: When I take the time to look at you
 from different perspectives to welcome your strangeness
 into my consciousness
 I am both rewarded and confused.
 But I still have a wall to build. Any suggestions?

Rock: No. I don't know how you can solve the dilemma of
 both reverencing and utilizing, but I know
 that once you have welcomed me into your awareness
 you will not be so simple-minded as to suppose rocks and
 trees exist only to trip you or as raw materials for
 constructing walls and houses . . .

Sam Keen
To A Dancing God

WASTE AND WISH

I love all waste
And solitary places; where we taste
The pleasure of believing what we see
Is boundless, as we wish our souls
 be.

Shelley

ALL I WANTED
WAS TO SING

When I was in first grade
I loved to sing.
When it was my turn I'd stand up
and sing clearly and happily,
thoroughly enjoying myself.
My teacher declared me singing champion . . .

Why did something as innocent and joyful
as the music of small children
have to be turned into a contest?
The voices should have been
sources of joy, not pride or shame.
But my first grade teacher thought
that my talent should be brandished
in front of my peers . . .

My joy became a mixture
of pride and shame,
and as time went on
shame overshadowed pride . . .
My teacher was the one who wanted
a champion;
all I wanted was to sing.

Mary Wilke
in *Seen Through Our Eyes*

DISTORTION

Sweet is the lore which Nature brings;
Our meddling intellect
Mis-shapes the beauteous forms of things;
We murder to dissect.

William Wordsworth

MAN UNBOUND

To play is to yield oneself
to a kind of magic . . .
to give the lie
to the inconvenient world of fact.

In play, earthly realities
become, of a sudden,
things of transient moment . . .
the mind is prepared
to accept the unimagined and incredible,
to enter a world where different laws apply,
to be relieved of all the weights
that bear it down,
to be free, kingly, unfettered and divine.

Hugo Rahner
Man At Play

In the light of this description of play
it becomes clear
that in several ways play and prayer
are strikingly similar.

Both are acts of disciplined fantasy.
In both we "yield to a kind of magic".
Neither prayer nor play
is limited or circumscribed by the
"inconvenient world of fact".
Both go beyond it.

Harvey Cox
A Feast of Fools

THE READINESS
TO RELISH

Festivity and contemplation
are close cousins.
The things that make life contemplative
are the same things
that make life celebrative: the capacity
to step back from tasks and chores,
the ability to "hang-lose"
from merely material goals,
the readiness to relish an experience
on its own terms.

Harvey Cox
A Feast Of Fools

REBIRTH

A funny thing happened to me
    in the carwash the other day—
        I felt like praying,
        During the pre-wash rites
I was unaware of the profound experience awaiting me,
    antagonistic, begrudging the time.
I did take note of the dismal day polluted with smog,
        the line-up of grim clouded faces—
        grimy, drab cars.

But the moment the left front wheel grooved
    into the automated track rolling me forward,
    I felt a blessed sense of release.
Obeying the instructions of my last human contact,
        an intense individual,
        I shut the windows tight,
        slipped into neutral—
threw both hands free of the steering wheel.
A complete sense of freedom from responsibility and
    a beautiful isolation enveloped me.
        White bubbles frothed
        and danced on every side.

Strange—my radio still brought music in
    oh, so very clearly
    from an outside world somewhere.
Pure fresh waters tumbled over the windows outside—
        Down, down—profligate streams
        of divinely-shaped rivulets.

It was then I felt like praying.
        It was all so clean
        so perfectly secluded
        so peacefully alone.
It was a purifying ritual—within and without . . .

Shiny, immaculate—my machine and I came forth.
In three minutes I had changed.
        It was the joy of the thing!
        The patterns!
        The colors!
        The rhythms!
Somehow in that crazy, utilitarian, technological
    happening, a fresh spirit of awe and surprise
    that I had known only as a child
                was reborn.

Rochonne Abrams
The Living Light

CELEBRATION

Life is full of surprises;
wonder at life is an experience
of one's total person and
calls for celebration . . .

Celebration involves
wonder
as insight into life,
festivity
as the affirmation of this insight, and
fantasy
of how life might be because of this insight . . .

The sensational
can easily generate wonder;
the commonplace can do likewise.
A sparrow can cause as much wonder
as the scarlet tanager;

ordinary walking, as much as . . .
walking on the moon.
In every case, there is the insight into life
which is far more than an intellectual appreciation . . .
Wonder is the most basic ingredient of
celebration . . .

Harvey Cox . . .
speaks of three elements of festivity:
excess, affirmation of life, and juxtaposition.
People go too far in festive moods . . .
and feel it the next morning.
Festivity always allows a short vacation
from the . . . conventional and stuffy.
Without some infraction of
the more structured formulas of daily life,
festivity would not be festivity.
Excess, going beyond the limits of daily life,
always characterizes festivity . . .

The second element is the affirmation of life . . .
Excess without the affirmation of life
is just plain excess and brings no
new insight into life.
Joy in the presence of sorrow,
life in the midst of death,
is festivity.
It is not so strange that the Vienna Orchestra
continued to play as the Germans
marched into the city;
they would be festive and affirm life
in the midst of
what would soon be death for so many . . .

The final element . . . is juxtaposition . . .
There has to be contrast;
no one can be festive all the time.
Without the winter,
who could appreciate the spring;
without the cold bleakness of January . . .
April would not be noticed.
Without 364 non-birthdays,
the one birthday would lose all its glitter . . .

Wonder drives us back into time
even as it happens now;
wonder makes us aware of how things are
and how things have been
if we merely open our eyes.
Festivity also happens now with an emphasis
on the present and without worry . . .
of yesterday and tomorrow.
Without some future orientation, however,
wonder brings no lasting effect;
without a future, festivity is running away.
What ushers in the future is fantasy:
how things might be . . .

It is not so strange
that the *Oxford History of the American People*
should end with the notes and lyrics from Camelot:
"Don't let it be forgot that once there was a spot,
For one brief shining moment,
that was known as Camelot."

Perhaps both Camelot and
the oblique reference to the Kennedy years
are both past orientated,
but in reality they are future orientated:
how things might be,
even if they never were in the past.
Take away fantasy,
and there will be little enthusiasm for life . . .
Things might be so different.

John F. O'Grady
"Celebration: What's it all About"

IMPULSE TO CELEBRATE

In contemplation one returns to
an object that was given in wonder
in order to prolong admiration and
appreciation:

a favorite stretch of beach,
a painting which has already
given hours of enjoyment,
the face of one long loved,
a familiar tree . . .

Out of such admiration grows
gratitude and the impulse to celebrate,
or possibly even to worship.
This response, however, brings us to
the threshold
of the experience of the holy.

Sam Keen
Apology For Wonder

CELEBRATE

Roar, sea, and all creatures in you;
    sing, earth, and all who live there!
Clap your hands, oceans;
    hills, sing together with joy
before the Lord . . .

Psalm 98:7-8

What a wonderful day
    the Lord has given us;
    let us be happy, let us celebrate . . .

Psalm 117:24

Start the music and play the tambourines;
    play pleasant music on the harps
    and the lyres.
Blow the horn for the festival . . .

Psalm 81:1-3

Praise the Lord . . .

Praise him with trumpets!
    Praise him with harps and lyres!
Praise him with drums and dancing . . .

Praise the Lord!

Psalm 150:1,3,6

WHAT MAKES LIFE LIVE?

You will never know
    what life means till you die:
Even throughout life
    'tis death that makes life live,
Give it whatever the significance.

Robert Browning

WHEN DREAMS GO

If a man could pass through Paradise
in a dream,
and have a flower presented to him as a pledge
that his soul had really been there,
and if he found
that flower in his hand when he awoke—
Ay! and what then?

Samuel Taylor Coleridge
Selected Poetry & Prose

UNSKIPPABLE STEPS

The contemplative insight is not
a product of human industry and genius,
although human preparation and participation
are unskippable steps
toward the center where the insight occurs,
where the gift is received—
the mystical experienced.

William McNamara
"The Heart of Religion"

MUTE WITNESS

Has not every man,
at one time in his life,
climbed a high hill and surveyed
the quilt of woodlands, fields, and houses
and asked himself: "Why all this?"
Where did it come from? What is it for?

Why the new calf walking with its mother?
Why the fiery sun warming the new-plowed fields?
Why the daisies, budding along the fence?
Why this world: being born, growing, dying?
Does it tell me something of the secret
that shadows my own existence?

But hardly before the question forms,
the flower stems and wheat blades point skyward.
But the fiery sun in one corner,
and the endless expanse of blue in the other,
refuse to yield up their secret.
But what they do say
tells me enough.

Dreams are the best evidence
that we are not as firmly
shut in our skins as we believe.

Friedrich Hebbel

Hold fast to dreams
For if dreams die
Life is a broken-winged bird
That cannot fly.

Hold fast to dreams
For when dreams go
Life is a barren field
Frozen with snow.

Langston Hughes

IN THE STILLNESS
IS THE DANCING

Nothing worth doing is completed
in our lifetime,
therefore we must be saved by hope.

Nothing true or beautiful makes complete sense
in any context of history,
therefore we must be saved by faith.

Nothing we do, no matter how virtuous,
can be accomplished alone,
therefore we are saved by love.

Reinhold Niebuhr

HOPE . . .

I hope that I will always be for each man
    what he needs me to be.
I hope that each man's death will diminish me,
    but fear of my own
    will never diminish my joy of life.
I hope that my love for those whom I like
    will never lessen my love
    for those whom I do not.
I hope that another man's love for me
    will never be a measure of my love for him.

I hope that every man will accept me as I am,
    but that I never will.
I hope that I will always ask for forgiveness from others,
    but will never need to be asked for my own.
I hope that I will always recognize my limitations,
    but that I will construct none.
I hope that loving will always be my goal,
    but that love will never be my idol.
I hope that every man will always have hope.

College student, quoted by
Henri J. M. Nouwen
Intimacy

NO BIRDS THIS YEAR

Take a deep breath of life
and consider how it should be lived . . .
Call nothing your own
except your soul.
Love not what you are,
but only what you may become.

Do not pursue pleasure
for you may have the misfortune
to overtake it.
Look always forward:
in last year's nest, there are no birds
this year.

Don Quixote
The Man From La Mancha

BEAUTIFUL WORLD

You are a child of the universe,
no less than the trees and the stars;
you have a right to be here.
And whether or not it is clear to you,
no doubt the universe is unfolding as it should.

Therefore be at peace with God,
whatever you conceive Him to be,
and whatever your labors and aspirations,
in the noisy confusion of life
keep peace with your soul.
With all its sham, drudgery and broken dreams,
it is still a beautiful world.

Desiderata

NEVER FORGET

Sing for joy to the Lord,
    all the world . . .
Never forget that the Lord is God!
    He made us, and we belong to him;
    we are his people . . .

Psalm 100:1,3

Praise his glorious name forever,
    and may his glory
    fill the whole earth!

Psalm 72:5,19

STAR PACE

Let us be like a bird for a moment perched
    On a frail branch while he sings;
Though he feels it bend, yet he sings his song,
    Knowing that he has wings.

Victor Hugo
"Wings"

Though my soul may set in darkness,
    it will rise in perfect light,
I have loved the stars too fondly
    to be fearful of the night.

Sarah Williams
"The Old Astronomer"

Who walks with Beauty has no need of
    fear;
The sun and moon and stars keep pace
    with him.

David Morton

CANTICLE OF THE SUN

O most high, almighty, good Lord God,
to you belong praise, glory, honor, and all blessing.

Praised be my Lord God with all his creatures,
and especially our brother the sun,
who brings us the day and
who brings us the night; fair is he and
shines with a very great splendor;
O Lord, he signifies you to us.

Praised be my Lord for our sister the moon,
and for the stars, which he has set clear and
lovely in the heaven.

Praised be my Lord for our brother the wind,
and for the air, and clouds, calms and
all weather by which you uphold life in all creatures.

Praised be my Lord for our sister water,
who is very serviceable to us and humble and
precious and very clean.

Praised be my Lord for our brother fire,
through whom you give us light in the darkness;
he is bright and pleasant and very mighty and strong.

Praised be my Lord for our mother the earth,
which sustains us and keeps us, and brings forth
grass and diverse fruits and flowers of many colors.

Praise and bless the Lord, and give thanks to him
and serve him with great humility.

St. Francis of Assisi

4

Be the Dream

SOUL

LOST HORIZON

Men go forth to wonder
at the height of mountains,
the huge waves of the sea,
the broad flow of the ocean,
the course of the stars —
and forget
to wonder at themselves.

Augustine
Confessions X 15

WE FORGET

We ask for a piece of sand
and he gives us a beach.

We ask for a drop of water
and he gives us an ocean.

We ask for time
and he gives us life eternal.

And it is so easy for us
to fall in love with the gift
and forget the giver.

Edward Farrell
Prayer is A Hunger

LIFE STYLE

Contemplation means different things
to different people.
At its narrowest,
it suggests a discipline for achieving
a particular state of consciousness . . .

In its wider sense, however . . .
contemplation is a way of life.
It is a basic attitude toward things . . .
According to the broader view,
the contemplative life may require
periods of withdrawal and use of
established techniques of meditation
in some stages,
but basically it is a life that can be lived
anywhere.
It is a way of being, a style of existence.

Harvey Cox
A Feast Of Fools

DIFFERENT

People think differently today
than they did in years past.
The communications explosion
has changed things.

A student with a transistor on a beach
can hear more different composers in a day
than Bach heard in a lifetime.

A housewife touring an art museum
can see more masterpieces in an hour
than Reubens saw in a year.

A business man reading *Newsweek* or *Time*
on a commuter is exposed to more news
in 10 minutes than
medieval man encountered
in 10 years.

This has had an effect on us.
In moments of reflection we wonder,
are we gaining touch with the world
at the expense of losing touch
with ourselves?

NOLI TIMERE

We must try to penetrate our most secret self, and examine our being from all sides. Let us try, patiently, to perceive the ocean of forces to which we are subjected and in which our growth is, as it were, steeped. This is a salutary exercise; for the depth and universality of our dependence on so much altogether outside our control all go to make up the embracing intimacy of our communion with the world to which we belong.

. . . And so, for the first time in my life perhaps (although I am supposed to meditate every day!), I took the lamp and, leaving the zone of everyday occupations and relationships where everything seems clear, I went down into my inmost self, to the deep abyss whence I feel dimly that my power and action emanates.

But as I moved further and further away from the conventional certainties by which social life is superficially illuminated, I became aware that I was losing contact with myself. At each step of the descent a new person was disclosed within me of whose name I was no longer sure, and who no longer obeyed me. And when I had to stop my exploration because the path faded from beneath my steps, I found a bottomless abyss at my feet, and out of it came—arising I know not from where—the current which I dare to call *my* life . . .

Stirred by my discovery, I then wanted to return to the light of day and forget the disturbing enigma in the comfortable surroundings of familiar things—to begin living again at the surface without imprudently plumbing the depths of the abyss. But then, beneath this very spectacle of the turmoil of life, there reappeared, before my newly-opened eyes, the unknown that I wanted to escape.

This time it was not hiding at the bottom of an abyss; it disguised its presence in the innumerable strands which form the web of chance, the very stuff of which the universe and my own small individuality are woven. Yet it was the same mystery without a doubt: I recognized it.

Our mind is disturbed when we try to plumb the depth of the world beneath us. But it reels still more when we try to number the favourable chance which must coincide at every moment if the leas of living things is to survive and to succeed in it enterprises.

After the consciousness of being something othe and something greater than myself—a second thin made me dizzy: namely, the supreme improbability the tremendous unlikelihood of finding myself ex

70

BE THE DREAM

Solitude enables you
to make contact with yourself,
a necessity if you want to realize yourself —
not to repeat like a parrot
a few acquired formulas,
but to be the prophet of God within you
who speaks a unique language
to each man.

Antonin Sertillanges
The Intellectual Life

isting in the heart of a world that has survived and succeeded in being a world.

At that moment, as anyone else will find who cares to make this same interior experiment, I felt the distress characteristic to a particle adrift in the universe, the distress which makes human wills flounder daily under the crushing number of living things and of stars. And if something saved me, it was hearing the voice . . . speaking to me from the depth of the night: *ego sum, noli timere* (It is I, be not afraid).

Teilhard de Chardin
The Divine Milieu

BEYOND COMPREHENSION

You created every part of me;
you put me together in my mother's womb . . .
You saw my bones being formed,
carefully put together in my mother's womb,
when I was growing in secret.

You saw me before I was born.
The days that had been created for me

had all been recorded in your book,
before any of them had ever begun.

God, how difficult your thoughts are for me;
how many of them there are!
If I counted them, they would be more
than the grains of sand.
When I awake, I am still with you.

Psalm 139:13-18

WATER THE EARTH
WITH TEARS OF JOY

The vault of heaven, full of soft, shining stars,
stretched vast and fathomless above him.
The Milky Way ran in two pale streams
from the zenith to the horizon . . .
The silence of the earth
seemed to melt into the silence of the heavens,
The mystery of earth was one
with the mystery of the stars . . .

Alyosha stood, gazed and suddenly
threw himself down on the earth.
He did not know why he embraced it . . .
But he kissed it weeping, sobbing and
watering it with his tears,
and vowed passionately to love it,
to love it forever and ever.
"Water the earth with tears of joy
and love those tears," echoed in his soul.
What was he weeping over?

Oh! in his rapture
he was weeping even over those stars,
which were shining to him from the abyss of space,
and "he was not ashamed of that ecstasy."
There seemed to be threads
from all those innumerable worlds of God,
linking his soul to them,
and it was trembling all over
"in contact with other worlds."
He longed to forgive everyone for everything,
and to beg forgiveness.
Oh, not for himself, but for all men,
for all and for everything.
"And others are praying for me, too,"
echoed again in his soul.

But with every instant, he felt clearly and,
as it were, tangibly,
that something firm and unshakeable
as that vault of heaven had entered into his soul.
It was as though some idea had seized
the sovereignty of his mind —
and it was for all his life and for ever and ever.
He had fallen on the earth a weak boy,
but he rose up a resolute champion,
and he knew and felt it suddenly
at the moment of his ecstacy.
And never, never, all his life long,
could Alyosha forget that minute.

Fyodor Dostoyevsky
The Brothers Karamozov

ALL IN ALL

Where could I go to escape your Spirit?
Where could I get away from your presence?
If I went up to heaven, you would be there;
if I lay down in the world of the dead,
you would be there

If I flew away beyond the east,
or lived in the farthest place in the west,
you would be there to lead me,
you would be there to help me.

I could ask the darkness to hide me,
or the light around me to turn into night,
but even the darkness is not dark for you,
and the night is as bright as the day.
Darkness and light are the same to you.

Psalm 139:7-12

JOY UNLIMITED

When I was young, I loved to skate.
Once the river in my hometown was solidly frozen.
I spent every free minute on the ice.

As my body glided effortlessly, it seemed I was
carving handwriting on the mirrorlike surface.
After I had practiced ardently for hours,
all restraint fell away,
and the smooth shift of balance brought with it
a sense of weightlessness.

The joy of life
that flowed through me in those days
has never been forgotten.

Magda Proskauer
"Breathing Therapy"

FOREVER

I have asked the Lord for one thing;
one thing only do I want:
to live in the Lord's house all my life . . .
Psalm 27:4

DISCOVERY

We stumbled on in the darkness,
over big stones and through large puddles,
along the one road leading from camp.
The accompanying guards kept shouting at us
and driving us with butts of their rifles . . .

Occasionally I looked at the sky,
where the stars were fading
and the pink light of the morning
was beginning to spread
behind a dark bank of clouds.
But my mind clung to my wife's image,
imagining it with an uncanny acuteness.
I heard her answering me,
saw her smile, her frank encouraging look.
Real or not, her look was more luminous
than the sun which was beginning to rise.

A thought transfixed me:
for the first time in my life I saw the truth
as it is set into song by so many poets,
proclaimed as the final wisdom by so many thinkers.
The truth—that love is the ultimate and
the highest goal to which man can aspire.
Then I grasped the meaning of the greatest secret
that human poetry and human thought and belief
have to impart:
The salvation of man is through love and in love.
I understood how a man who has nothing left
in this world still may know bliss,
be it only for a brief moment,
in the contemplation of his beloved . . .
For the first time in my life I was able to
understand the meaning of the words,
"The angels are lost in perpetual contemplation
of an infinite glory."

Viktor Frankl
Man's Search For Meaning

BRINK OF WONDER

Whenever beauty overwhelms us,
whenever wonder
silences our chattering hopes
and worries,
we are close to worship.

Richard C. Cabot
What Men Live By

NEW BORN

One day, a few days after the liberation,
I walked through the country
past flowering meadows, for miles and miles,
toward the market town near the camp.
Larks rose to the sky
and I could hear their joyous song.
There was no one to be seen for miles around;
there was nothing but the wide earth and sky
and the larks' jubilation and the freedom of space.

I stopped, looked around, and up to the sky—
and then I went down on my knees.
At that moment there was very little I knew
of myself or of the world—
I had but one sentence in mind—always the same:
"I called to the Lord from my narrow prison
and He answered me in the freedom of space."

How long I knelt there and repeated this sentence
memory can no longer recall.
But I know that on that day, in that hour,
my new life started.
Step for step I progressed,
until I again became a human being.

Viktor Frankl
Man's Search For Meaning

77

EXPLORING PEAKS

Apparently most people, or almost all people,
have peak experiences, or ecstasies.
The question might be asked in terms of
the single most joyous, happiest,
most blissful moment of your whole life . . .

How did you feel different about yourself at that time?
How did the world look different?
What did you feel like?
What were your impulses?
How did you change if you did?

Abraham Maslow
The Farther Reaches of Human Nature

PRICELESS

It seems to me
"that this separateness of individuals,
the right of each individual to utilize
his experience in his own way
and to discover his own meanings in it—
this is one of the most
priceless potentialities of life.

Carl R. Rogers
On Becoming A Person

WAITING WITHIN

Our experiences
are not things that are past and gone.
Rather, they lie deep within—asleep,
waiting to be awakened,
waiting to be called forth
from the depths of unconsciousness.

When was I happiest and
most at peace with myself in life?
Why did I experience such peace?

When was the last time I felt
a higher presence in my life?
Or did I ever?

When was the last time I felt
deeply dejected—out of touch with
goodness and beauty?
Or am I too "closed in" on myself
that I cannot reach out?

When was the last time I experienced
the deep joy of helping another,
or in sharing myself completely with
someone or something?

ONE MORE BOUNCE?

I used to walk down the streets . . .
and suddenly would break out in a cold sweat.
I thought I might be losing my mind.
One day it was so bad that I got in my company car
and took off . . .

As I was driving through the tall pine wood country
of East Texas I suddenly pulled up beside the road
and stopped.
I remember sitting there in complete despair.
I had always had the feeling that there was
"one more bounce in the ball."
After . . . a couple of martinis and a good night's sleep,
one could always start again tomorrow.
But now there was no tomorrow in my situation.
I was like a man on a great gray treadmill . . .

As I sat there I began to weep like a little boy,
which I suddenly realized I was inside.
I looked up toward the sky.
There was nothing I wanted to do with my life.
And I said, "God, if there's anything you want
in this stinking soul, take it."

[T]his was almost ten years ago.
But something came into my life that day
which has never left.
There wasn't any . . . flashing lights or visions;
but it was a deep intuitive realization of what it is
God wants from a man which I had never known before.
And the peace which came with this understanding
was not an experience in itself, but rather
a cessation of the conflict of a lifetime.
I realized then that God does not want a man's money,
nor does He primarily want his time,
even the whole lifetime . . .
He wants your *will*; and if you give Him your will,
He'll begin to show you life as you've never seen it before.
It is like being born again . . .

As I sat there I continued to cry,
only now the tears were a release from a lifetime
of being bound by myself . . .
Although I could not understand nor articulate
for many months what had happened to me,
I knew to the core of my soul
that I had somehow made personal contact with
the very Meaning of Life.

I started the car and turned toward home.

Keith Miller
The Taste of New Wine

CLOTHES OF JOY

You have changed my sadness into
a joyful dance;
you have taken off my clothes of mourning,
and given me clothes of joy.

So I will not be silent;
I will sing praise to you.
Lord, you are my God,
I will give thanks to you forever.

Psalm 30:11-12

I ASKED THE BIG MAN

I went back to my cell . . .
The night before my hearing,
I decided to make a prayer.
It had to be on my knees . . .
I couldn't play it cheap.
So I waited until the thin kid was asleep,
then I quietly climbed down from my top bunk
and bent my knees . . .

I knelt at the foot of the bed
and told God what was in my heart.
I made like He was there in the flesh with me.
I talked to Him plain . . .
no big words, no almighties . . .
I talked to Him like I had wanted to talk
to my old man so many years ago.
I talked like a little kid and I told Him of
my wants and lacks, of my hopes and disappointments.
I asked the Big Man . . . to make a cool way for me . . .
I felt like I was someone
that belonged to somebody who cared.
I felt like I could even cry if I wanted to,
something I hadn't been able to do for years.
"God," I concluded, "maybe I won't be an angel,
but I do know I'll try not to be a blank.
So in Your name, and in *Cisto's* name, I ask this. Amen."

A small voice added another amen to mine.
I looked up and saw the thin kid, his elbows bent,
his head resting on his hand.
I peered through the semidarkness to see his face,
wondering if he was sounding me.
But his face was like mine, looking for help from God.
There we were, he lying down,
head on bended elbows, and I still on my knees.
No one spoke for a long while.
Then the kid whispered,
"I believe in *Dios* also.
Maybe you don't believe it, but I used to go to church,
and I had the hand of God on me.
I felt always like you and I feel now, warm,
quiet, and peaceful,
like there's no suffering in our hearts."

"What's it called, *Chico*, this what we feel?"
I asked softly.

"It's Grace by the Power of the Holy Spirit,"
the kid said.

I didn't ask any more.
There, in the semidarkness,
I had found a new sense of awareness . . .

Piri Thomas
Down These Mean Streets

JOY IN THE MORNING

I cried to you for help, Lord my God,
and you healed me.
You brought me back from the world of
the dead.
I was with those who go down to the
depths below, but you restored my life . . .

There may be tears during the night,
but joy comes in the morning.

Psalm 30:2-5

ONLY BY LOVE

I was returning from hunting
and walking along an avenue of the garden,
my dog running in front of me.

Suddenly he took shorter steps,
and began to steal along
as though tracking game.

I looked along the avenue,
and saw a young sparrow . . .
It had fallen out of the nest . . .
and sat unable to move,
helplessly flapping its half-grown wings.

My dog was slowly approaching it,
when suddenly
darting from a tree close by,
an old dark-throated sparrow
fell like a stone right before his nose,
and all ruffled up, terrified . . .
flung itself twice towards
the open jaws of shining teeth.

It sprang to save;
it cast itself before its nestling . . .
but all its tiny body was shaking with terror . . .
Swooning with fear, it offered itself up!

What a huge monster
must the dog have seemed to it!
And yet it could not stay
on its high branch out of danger . . .
A force stronger than its will flung it down . . .

I hastened to call off the disconcerted dog,
and went away, full of reverence . . .

Love, I thought,
is stronger than death or fear of death.
Only by it, by love, life holds together and advances.

Ivan Turgenev
Poems in Prose

INTEGRATING EXPERIENCE

He who neglects to drink
of the spring of experience
is apt to die of thirst
in the desert of ignorance.

Ling Po

If you integrate your awareness,
and unify your thoughts,
spirit will make its abode
with you.

Chuang-tzu

SEARCH FOR A PIVOT

From my earliest childhood
the need to possess some "absolute"
was the pivot of all my inner life.
Amid the pleasures that surrounded me at this age,
I was (I remember it vividly) happy only when
I felt *fundamental* joy which, in general, consisted in
the possession (or the thought) of some object
sensed to be more precious, more consistent,
and more unalterable than any other.

Sometimes it was just a piece of metal;
or again, leaping to the other extreme,
I would take delight in the thought of God/Spirit
(at the time, the Flesh of Christ
seemed to me too fragile, too corruptible).

. . . I had at that time an irresistible need
(both life-giving and consoling) to come to rest forever
in something tangible and definite.
And I searched everywhere for this beatifying Object.
The story of my inner life is summed up in this search,
ever dwelling on realities
more and more universal and perfect.
Fundamentally this deep natural tendency has remained
absolutely unchanged ever since I began to know myself.

Teilhard de Chardin
quoted by Claude Tresmontant
in *Pierre Teilhard de Chardin*

"DREAM HID IN DREAM"

God guard me from those thoughts men think
In the mind alone;
He that sings a lasting song
Thinks in a marrow-bone . . .

William Butler Yeats
"A Prayer For Old Age"

God loves dim ways of glint and gleam;
To please him well my verse must be
A dyed and figured mystery;
Thought hid in thought, dream hid in dream.

William Butler Yeats

The most beautiful thing
we can experience
is the mystery.

Albert Einstein

ULTIMATE EXPERIENCE

To see the world in a Grain of Sand
And Heaven in a Wild Flower,
Hold Infinity in the palm of your hand
And Eternity in an hour.

William Blake

I can see nothing plain; all's mystery.
Yet sometimes there's a torch inside my head
That makes all clear, but when the light is gone
I have but images, analogies.

William Butler Yeats

5

New Wine

TRANSFORMATION

MYSTICAL PARADOX

Man's contemplative pursuit
of ultimate reality
leads inevitably
to a mysterious threshold.

Try as he may,
mortal man never succeeds
in fully crossing it.

Even those mystics/prophets,
who were gifted
with some fractional insight
into the mystery,
could never really comprehend—
much less communicate—
what they experienced.

When reflecting upon it later,
they either despaired of words, or
resorted to a mystical symbolism
that mirrored
a paradox of trembling and fascination.

"I FELL PRONE . . ."

Then he led me to the gate
which faces the east, and there
I saw the glory of the God of Israel
coming from the east.
I heard a sound
like the roaring of many waters,
and the earth shone with his glory . . .

I fell prone as the glory of the Lord
entered the temple by way of the gate
which faces the east,
but the spirit lifted me up
and brought me to the inner court.
And I saw that the temple was filled
with the glory of the Lord.

Ezeckiel 43:1-5

ELIJAH HID HIS FACE

Elijah came to a cave, where he took shelter . . .
Then the Lord said,
"Go outside and stand on the mountain before the Lord;
the Lord will be passing by."

A strong and heavy wind was rending the mountains
and crushing rocks before the Lord—
but the Lord was not in the wind.
After the wind there was an earthquake—
but the Lord was not in the earthquake.
After the earthquake there was fire—
but the Lord was not in the fire.
After the fire there was a tiny whispering sound.
When he heard this,
Elijah hid his face in his cloak
and went and stood at the entrance of the cave.

I Kings 19:9,11-13

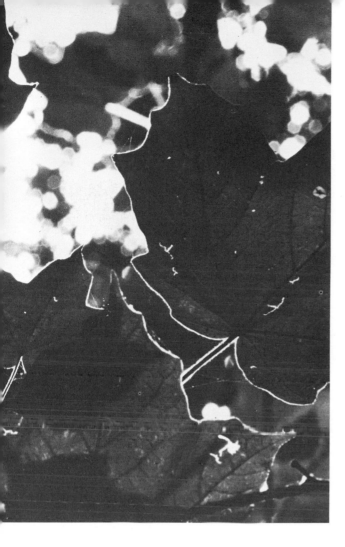

THE FRAME SHOOK

I saw the Lord seated on a high and lofty throne,
with the train of his garment
filling the temple.
Seraphim were stationed above;
each of them had six wings;
with two they veiled their faces,
with two they veiled their feet, and
with two they hovered aloft.

"Holy, holy, holy,
is the Lord of hosts!" they cried one to the other.
"All the earth is filled with his glory!"

At the sound of that cry,
the frame of the door shook and
the house was filled with smoke.

Isaiah 6:1-4

"COME NO NEARER!"

God called out to him from the bush,
"Moses! Moses!"

He answered, "Here I am."

God said, "Come no nearer!
Remove the sandals from your feet,
for the place where you stand is
holy ground.
I am the God of your father . . ."
Moses hid his face, for he was afraid
to look at God.

Exodus 3:1-7

"LISTEN TO HIM!"

Jesus took
Peter, James, and John with him,
and led them up a high mountain
by themselves.
As they looked on,
a change came over him,
and his clothes
became very shining and white . . .

Peter . . . and the others
were so frightened
that they did not know what to say.
A cloud appeared
and covered them with its shadow,
and a voice came from the clouds:
"This is my own dear Son —
listen to him!"

Mark 9:2-7

UNCERTAIN SHADOW

Left to human resources,
even prophets and mystics
grapple with the mystery
"beyond"
in almost total blindness.

They grope toward it —
and from it —
only in uncertain shadow.

NEW WINE

When the day of Pentecost arrived,
all the believers
gathered together in one place.
Suddenly there was
a great noise from the sky
which sounded like
a strong wind blowing, and . . .
they saw what looked like
tongues of fire spreading out; and . . .
they were all filled with the Holy Spirit . . .

There were Jews living in Jerusalem . . .
who had come from
every country in the world.
When they heard this noise,
a whole crowd gathered.
They were all excited,
because each one of them heard the believers
talking in his own language . . .

Amazed and confused
they all kept asking each other,
"What does this mean?"

Acts of the Apostles 2:1-12

In the past
God spoke to our ancestors
many times in many ways through
the prophets,
but in these last days he has
spoken to us through his Son.

Hebrews 1:1

TRANSFORMED

And that is how Theology started.
People already knew about God in a vague way.
Then came a man who claimed to be God;
and yet He was not the sort of man
you could dismiss as a lunatic.
He made them believe Him.

They met Him again
after they had seen Him killed.

And then after they had been formed
into a little society or community,
they found God somehow inside them as well:
directing them,
making them able to do things
they could never do before.

C. S. Lewis
Mere Christianity

JESUS

It is to Jesus, then,
that we must turn for clarity
concerning the ultimate mystery of life.

He shines
with the brightness of God's glory;
he is the exact likeness
of God's own being.

Hebrews 1:3

[W]e must think of the Son always,
so to speak,
streaming forth from the Father,
like light from a lamp,
or heat from a fire,
or thoughts from a mind.

He is the self-expression of the Father—
what the Father has to say.
And there never was a time
when He was not saying it.

C. S. Lewis
Mere Christianity

ULTIMATE REVELATION

In Jesus Christ the reality of God
entered into the reality of the world.
The . . . answer . . .
both to the question concerning
the reality of God
and to the question concerning
the reality of the world,
is designated solely and alone by the name
Jesus Christ . . .

Henceforward one can speak
neither of God nor the world
without speaking of Jesus Christ.

Dietrich Bonhoeffer
Ethics

O world invisible, we view thee,
O world intangible, we touch thee,
O world unknowable, we know thee.

Francis Thompson

THE INCARNATE WORD

Something which has existed since the beginning,
that we have heard,
and we have seen with our own eyes;
that we have watched
and touched with our hands:
the Word, who is life—
this is our subject . . .

What we have seen and heard
we are telling you
so that you may be in union with us,
as we are in union
with the Father
and with his Son Jesus Christ.
We are writing this to you to make our own joy
complete.

John 1:1-4

GOD'S WORD

Whether we are believers or not,
when we read the Gospels
we are reading a book in which,
according to its authors,
it is God—rather than man—
who speaks to us from its pages:

Have faith in God and faith in me . . .
I am the way, the truth, and the life . . .

John 14:1

The words I have spoken to you
are Spirit and life.

John 6:63

I am the resurrection and the life . . .
whoever believes in me will never die.

John 11:25

ALL SHOUT "GLORY"

The Lord's voice is heard on the seas;
   the glorious God thunders,
   and his voice echoes over the ocean . . .

The Lord's voice breaks the cedars,
   even the cedars of Lebanon.
He causes the mountains of Lebanon
   to jump like calves,
   and Mount Hermon to leap like a young bull.

The Lord's voice makes the lightning flash.
His voice makes the desert shake . . .
The Lord's voice makes the deer give birth,
   and leaves the trees stripped bare,
   while in his temple
   all shout, "Glory to God!"

Psalm 29:3-9

TO EVERY PART

The Father himself loves you.
He loves you because you love me
and have believed I came from God.

John 16:27

Father! May they be in us,
just as you are in me
and I am in you.
May they be one . . .
that the world may know that you
sent me and
that you love them as you love me.

John 17:21-23

Christ has shown himself among us.
God has made his dwelling place
in the midst of us.
The voice of peace has spoken . . .
and love has reached every part.

Syrian Rite

TRANSFORMING POWER

The message of the Bible is . . .
that into the confusion of man's world,
with its divisions and hatred,
has come a message
of transforming power,
and those who believe it
will experience within themselves
the power
that makes for reconciliation and
peace on earth . . .

Thomas Merton
"Opening the Bible"

JOY

Many prophets and holy men
longed to see what you see,
and never saw it;

to hear what you hear,
and never heard it.

Matthew 13:17

NEW BIRTH

The word of God . . .
penetrating our inmost being
is more than
a communication of light:

it is a new birth,
the beginning of a new being.

Thomas Merton
"Opening the Bible"

OPEN AMAZEMENT

The Christian's reaction
of awe and wonder of God
comes not from contemplating
God's majesty and glory,
but from realizing the incredible fact
that God is authentically related to us
in love.

Our reaction of awe
stems from the overwhelming realization
that God is interested in us, and that,
this "ultimate mystery" of life
is enmeshed personally in human history.

Insofar as this realization clarifies
in our minds
verbalized prayer tends to recede;
prayer becomes mute, open amazement—
pure worship.

As realization matures,
we begin to fathom even deeper implications.
We begin to see
that God's self-revelation to us involves also
a personal revelation about ourselves—
what we are, and what we are to become.

Christian prayer becomes
not only a reflective awareness and acceptance
of ultimate reality,
but also a reflective awareness and acceptance
of personal reality as well.
In its purest form,
Christian prayer becomes the mute, open
amazement—the awe and wonder—
that bursts forth and blooms
in the heart of the praying Christian.

SONG OF "BECOMING"

My soul takes wings when I behold
becoming things:
seeds in fullness,
gushing into greenness;
plants in budness,
bursting into bloomness;
blooms in beautifulness,
exploding into fruitfulness.
Seeds, plants, and blooms—
sing of becomingness.

Have we here a sign—
a paradigm for you and me?
Is humanity, in fullness
destined for newness?

Dare we chance our destiny—
dream/think to share divinity?

THE CHRIST LEAP

Thought balks/walks softly
when stalking mystery.
Who is this Christ:
strange blend, God-man meshed?

How view this bridge/marriage
linking quantum leaps?
In Christ, did human fullness
burst/fuse into newness?
In him, yet man, did the leap occur—
but stay meshed/unmasked
till Easter morn?
Was he the firstborn of the leap:
ripe humanity launching/exploding
into undreamed divinity?

Is he sheer mastery/mystery, or
sign/sacrament of our destiny?

QUANTUM LEAPS?

Does life progress in quantum leaps?
Was nonlife seed to life?
And plant life father to sense life?
Was sense life sire to conscious life?
If so, what quantum leap in life
lies yet unborn in the womb of conscious life?

What stirred/spurred the leaps of life?
And, now that life is conscious of itself,
is it master of its destiny—
free to father-forth another leap,
or abort the child in stillborn sleep?

Reason writhes, waits and wonders.
Faith denies the wait, exalts the wonder.
In Christ the quantum leap was born.
Divine life broke through on Easter morn.

END-POINT

Lord . . .
when it was given me to see
where the dazzling trail
of particular beauties
and partial harmonies was leading,
I recognized that it was all
coming to center on a single point,
a single person:
yourself . . .

Thus all the lines converge,
complete one another, interlock.
All things are now but one.

Teilhard de Chardin
Hymn of the Universe

PROBE CHALLENGE

The gospel invites us to believe in
Jesus and his message.
"These [things] are written," said John,
"that you may believe . . .
and that through this faith
you may have life in his name."

John 20:31

The gospel also invites us to reflect
on our personal lives.
It prods us to look at life more deeply.
It challenges us to probe beneath
apparent meanings to deeper meanings.
Jesus consistently invited the people
to search for the deeper meaning
underlying the events of their lives and times.

Jesus said:
"When you see a cloud
coming up in the west,
at once you say, 'It is going to rain,'
and it does . . .
You can look at the . . .
sky and tell what it means;
why, then, don't you know the meaning of
the present times?"

Luke 12:54-56

Jesus said:
"I am the light of the world.
Whoever follows me will have the light of life
and will not walk in darkness."

John 8:12

One way to illumine the deeper meaning
of the events of life is to expose them to
the "light" of Jesus' teachings in the Gospel.

HELL OF A PRAYER

The Rev. Richard L. Huggins, 30,
this week's "guest chaplain" in the
[Pennsylvania] Senate, began the session
with this prayer:

"Well, God, here we are again,
asking your help in another week
when we look at the frustrations and frenzy
in running a state.

The hell of it is, God, we are not sure
that we really want your help.
We feel self-sufficient. But we really are not.

Help us anyway.
Strengthen our minds and our abilities
for the commonwealth. Amen."

UPI News Story
Chicago Tribune

In your prayers do not use lots of words,
as the pagans do, who think that God will hear them
because of their long prayers.
Do not be like them; your Father already knows
what you need before you ask him.

Matthew 6:7-8

NO BANDS PLAYED

I do not believe the greatest threat
to our future
is from bombs or guided missiles.
I don't think our civilization will die that way.
I think it will die when we no longer care.
Arnold Toynbee has pointed out
that 19 of 21 civilizations have died from within
and not by conquest from without.
There were no bands playing and flags waving
when these civilizations decayed.
It happened slowly,
in the quiet and the dark
when no one was aware.

Lawrence M. Gould

You are like salt for all mankind.
But if salt loses its taste,
there is no way to make it salty again.
It has become worthless;
so it is thrown away and people walk on it.

Matthew 5:13

YOU CANNOT SEE IT

The average person in this country
is taxed over $400 for military expenses
and only slightly over $2.50
for food programs.

One main battle tank costs
full-time psychotherapy for 171 drug addicts
for one year.

One B-1 Bomber costs fifteen 50-bed
public hospitals.

One aircraft carrier costs 67,000
low cost housing units with two bedrooms each.

. . .

He came closer to the city and when he saw it
he wept over it, saying:
"If you only knew today what is needed for peace!
But now you cannot see it!"

Luke 19:41-42

WHO WILL RESCUE
THE ADULT?

William Golding's *Lord of the Flies*
depicts a group of British adolescents
who have reverted to savagery
after being marooned on an island.

Eventually, a British warship discovers the boys.
They come ashore
just in time to halt a savage manhunt.
The irony appears, however,
when the boys are removed to the warship,
whose crew is also involved in
stalking human beings.
"And who will rescue the adult from the carrier?"
asks Golding.

. . .

I don't do the good I want to do;
instead, I do the evil
that I do not want to do . . .

What an unhappy man I am!
Who will rescue me from this body
that is taking me to death?

Romans 7:19, 24

"WHAT THEN . . . ?"

I have a dream that one day
this nation will rise up and live out
the true meaning of its creed.
We hold these truths to be
self-evident
that all men are created equal.

I have a dream that one day
in the red hills of Georgia
the sons of former slaves and
the sons of former slave owners
will be able to sit down together
at the table of brotherhood . . .

This is our hope.
This is our faith that I go back
to the South with.
With this faith, we will be able to
hew out of the mountain of despair
a stone of hope.

Martin Luther King

Now Joseph had a dream . . .
And because of his dreams and words
they hated him the more . . .
They said to one another,
"Here comes that dreamer!
Let us therefore kill him . . .
Let us see then what becomes of his dreams."

Genesis 37:1, 8, 20

CRUCIBLE OF DIVERSITY

William Braden's, *The Age Of Aquarius* concerns,
what he calls, the "conflict of two cultures".
The one is orientated toward the sciences
and the other is orientated toward the humanities.

This conflict
"can be seen as a basic factor
in the Black Power movement; in the protest of the New Left;
in the supposed confusion of sexual roles;
in the development of an LSD subculture;
in the so-called Leap to the East;
by many drugstore disciples of Hinduism and Zen Buddhism;
in the current faddish enthusiasm for astrology,
witchcraft, and sensitivity training;
in anti-scientism; in the newly emerging emphasis on ecology,
environmental control, and the often mystical worship
of nature; in the reassertion of ethnicity;
in the now-defunct Death of God theology as well as
the newer attraction referred to as the Theology of Hope."

What is central to all these phenomena, argues Braden,
is the question of identity.
Like it or not, America is moving toward a new identity,
"a collective identity that will be blacker, more feminine,
more oriental, more emotional, more intuitive,
more exuberant — and, just possibly, better than the old one."

The new ontology will have to be one centered upon
what living in community means. Says Braden:
"This new generation has very often expressed empathy
for human suffering which somehow suggests a conviction
that there is a bond between man and man;
that there does exist some sort of universal identity;
that in some strange sense
we do each of us bleed when the other is cut."

What is needed is not lock-step homogeneity, but
a creative harmony forged in the crucible of diversity.

Adapted from
Peter J. Fleming's review
of "The Age of Aquarius:
Technology and the Cultural Revolution"

If the foot were to say, "Because I am not a hand,
I don't belong to the body," that would not make it
stop being a part of the body.
And if the ear were to say, "Because I am not an eye,
I don't belong to the body," that would not make it
stop being a part of the body . . .
God put every different part in the body just as he wished.
There would not be a body if it were all only one part!

1 Corinthians 12:15-19

SELF-FULFILLING
PROPHECY

Man has forgotten what he can do.
And because of this lapse of memory,
he has lost sight of what he can be.

"Self-fulfilling prophecy"—you hear
the word a lot these days.
It names a deep-down force in all of us
that plays a role in such varied fields
as politics, athletics, drama and
international relations.

It comes down to this, says a
Harvard psychologist:
"One person's prediction of
another person's behavior somehow
comes to be realized."

When trackman Roger Bannister
set out to break the 4 minute mile
few sportsmen thought he could do it.
Even Bannister was skeptical:
"At first I wasn't sure either," he said.
"But I knew my trainer believed in me,
and I couldn't let him down."

"All of us," says a noted sociologist,
"carry on a constant dialogue with ourselves.
We are constantly making predictions about
what we can and cannot do.
And there are few of us who could not
do a lot more
if we simply expected more of ourselves."

The apostles said to the Lord, "Make our faith greater."
The Lord answered: "If you had faith as big as a
mustard seed, you could say to this mulberry tree,
'Pull yourself up by the roots and plant yourself in the sea!'
and it would obey you."

Luke 17:5-6

103

ON-GOING

The day I decided to commit my life wholly to God
I scooped up everything I could see
above the level of my consciousness
and offered it to Christ. I felt free;
but then, several mornings later a hoary head
came up out of the slimy pool, an old resentment.

I was filled with discouragement
and I thought I must not have really committed
my life to God at all.
But then I realized joyously that of course I had—
that all a man does
when he commits his "whole life" is to commit
that of which he is conscious.
And according to many psychologists,
the major part of the human Psyche is below
the level of consciousness.

So the totally "committed Christian life"
is a life of continually committing one's self
and one's problems day by day
as they are slowly revealed to his own consciousness.

Keith Miller
The Taste of New Wine

Do not lose your courage . . .
We are not people who turn back and are lost.
Instead, we have faith and are saved.

Hebrews 10:35, 39

QUASARS

Engineers measure computer operations
in pico-seconds (trillionths of a second).

Astronomers say that the
most distant bodies from Earth, quasars,
are nine billion light-years away.

Medical men tell us that the brain cell
is connected to as many as
60,000 other cells.

Scientists estimate that as many as
one million planets in our Milky Way galaxy
could support not only primitive life,
but intelligent life.

Adapted from
Hi-Time

. . .

When I look at the sky, which you have made . .
what is man that you think of him;
mere man, that you care for him?

Psalm 8:3-4

LOST MELODIES

The books of Sacred Scripture
contain much more than
what is written in them.
Our soul also has depths
unknown to us.

On the sacred pages and in our soul,
there are melodies we do not hear.
In the spaces of the world
there are melodies which no one catches
because no one listens.

Eugenio Zolli
Before the Dawn

GOD'S GRANDEUR

The world is charged with the
  grandeur of God
    It will flame out, like
    shining from shook foil;
    It gathers to a greatness,
    like the ooze of oil
Crushed. Why do men then now
  not reck his rod?
Generations have trod, have trod,
  have trod;
    And all is seared with trade;
    bleared, smeared with toil;
    And wears man's smudge
    and shares man's smell:
    the soil

Is bare now, nor can foot feel, being
  shod.

And for all this, nature is never spent;
    There lives the dearest freshness
    deep down things;
And though the last lights off the black
  West went
    Oh, morning at the brown brink
    eastward, springs—
Because the Holy Ghost over the bent
  World broods with warm breast
  and with ah! bright wings.

Gerard Manley Hopkins
"God's Grandeur"

6

Join the Dancing

DARE REBIRTH

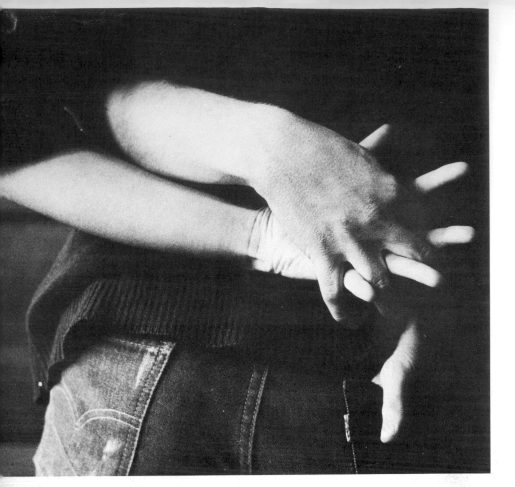

DISTANCE

I find myself endurable
only when
I can forget myself,
when
I can get away from myself
by prayer
and find my life in you.

Karl Rahner

DARE PRAYER

You pray
in your distress and
in your need;
would that you might pray
also
in the fullness of your joy and
in your days of abundance.

Kahlil Gibran

CHILL FACTOR

I realized
that in so much of my life
I had been a spiritual sensualist,
always wanting to *feel*
God's presence in my prayers . . .

I saw
that until I could believe
without spiritual goose pimples
I would always be . . .
at the mercy of my emotional feelings.

So I tried this praying
whether I felt spiritual or not;
and for the first time in my life found
that we *can* live
on raw faith.
I found that often
the very act of praying this way brings later
a closer sense of God's presence.

And I realized a strange thing:
that if a person in his praying
has the *feeling*,
he doesn't really need
the *faith*.

Keith Miller
The Taste of New Wine

SONG OR SILENCE

Prayer can be
a curse,
a cry,
a gesture,
a silence,
an acceptance of life,

a protest,
a folded hand,
an open palm,
a clenched fist,
a song,
a dour way of life;

but also:
caring for another,
thanking for love by giving love,
standing firm in humanity
in uncertainty
and doubt.

J. G. Jacobs

A TASTE OF WILDERNESS

If I am in sickness,
my sickness may serve Him;
if I am in sorrow,
my sorrow may serve Him.
He does nothing in vain,
He knows what He is about.

John Henry Newman

O, do not pray for easy lives.
Pray to be stronger men.
Do not pray for tasks equal to your powers.
Pray for powers equal to your tasks.

Phillip Brooks
Going Up To Jerusalem

No Christian escapes a taste
of the wilderness
on the way to the promised land.

Evelyn Underhill
The Fruits of the Spirit

DIFFERENT FORMULATIONS?

Is my life . . .
a single short aspiration
and all my prayers
just different formulations of it
in human words?

Karl Rahner

PRAYER FLIGHTS

Why am I so slow
to go all the way?
Why do I find it hard to work
without pay?

Lord, why am I this way?
Why can't I admit that
half-commitment is no commitment—
that it is like trying to walk,
but on only one leg;
like trying to sail
but without any wind?

Once someone accepted me—
me, with my somewhat long nose
and skinny features.
Someone accepted
the way I speak,
the way I act in public, and
the way I really am.

Because I was accepted,
I can see more clearly who I am
and accept myself without reservation
I no longer want to be another.

I am myself—simply and surely.
Love has finally defined for me
the man I really am, and always was.
And I am not troubled or ashamed
by this definition.

Please, God, never let me despair
because I am who I am.

God, sometimes
I turn away from you in despair
giving up all hope of understanding.
Why must you be so distant?
But forgive me, for I realize
that your greatness
is part of an ever-unfolding
mystery.

PRECISELY THE OPPOSITE

Man, caught up
in the whirl of ambition and
self-assertion
has lost
appreciation of the mystery,
wonder
and stillness of life.

He procrastinates
until he feels the urge to pray
and sometimes
the urge never comes.

Sometimes
he is only brought to prayer
because of some affliction
but then,
instead of realizing prayer,
he treats it
as a kind of psychotherapy,
something to get practical results
for himself.

Prayer is
precisely the opposite:
it is absence
of self-centered thought.

J. Massingberd Ford

Lord, it's morning!
Your sun—on easter feet—
has creeped into my room
and called me
from my slumber tomb:

"Arise, be risen,
and spread the news.
It's morning!"

God of after-sunset
God of half-light and almost night,
God of quiet and stillness,
God of coolness
    that drifts up from the river,
God of silhouetted leaves
    against a silvered sky,
God of singing crickets
    and blinking fireflies—
God of these, be my God, too.

111

AND WHY NOT?

If God
is anything more than mortal
he certainly has no need
to be reminded of
the needs of his creatures . . .

I can only make
several observations.

When I allow myself to pray . . .
I feel very differently
from when I am talking to myself.
I know
the feeling of interior dialogue.

In prayer
I feel my words going out
to the unknown mystery
which I trust
is the caring context of my existence.
I do not find myself
in communication with any person.
There are no answering words.

I find I must, on occasions,
bring my longing,
sorrow,
joy,
anxiety
to focus in words and
utter them to
the unknown source of my existence.
And why should I not?

Sam Keen
To A Dancing God

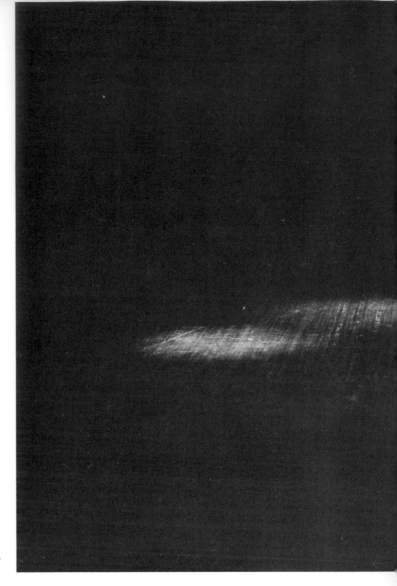

DEPTH EXPERIENCE

Authentic prayer
must come from
the heart, and not
the lips alone.
Perhaps, that's why
so many of us are moved
to pray
right after a depth-experience
of the heart:

the delight
of an unexpected surprise,
the death of a close friend,
the experience
of being really needed—
coupled with the painful awareness
of our limitation to meet the need—
the joy
of an intimate communication
with a friend
in a late-night conversation.

REALITY

Seated on a bunk, trying to hold rigid . . .
the broken neck of an elderly woman
whose survival depended on me,
I prayed for the first time
without feeling self-conscious about it.

Harlan Cleveland
"Affect the Farthest Star"

If God is for real, then a prayer
is about real people, real problems,
real gropings, real dreams and joys,
and for real occasions.

If God is love, then a prayer reflects
an atmosphere of basic trust,
and honesty unlimited, a giving of one's self . . .
as well as a confidence of forgiveness and
continued acceptance . . .

If God is for all people, then prayer
is so personal that you feel it is your own,
yet it is so universal
that it is meaningful for others too.

If God is the father of all creation,
then a prayer is our best thinking
about truth and the order of things.
And it reflects an assurance
that the way of a loving father for his children
is good and ultimately victorious.

Each prayer is different.
Each moment of meditation is different.
Each person is different.
But each prayer is an effort to tune in
to what God and life and you and I are all about.

Herman C. Ahrens, Jr.
Tune In

SHARED PRAYER

Sometimes a man
"wants to share his prayer
wants to share his life,
not just a sequence of events,
emotions and thoughts.
He wants to share a moment
in which the question of
the meaning of existence
can be raised.

Based on this conviction
some university students asked
their friends . . .
'Are you willing to write a prayer?' . . .
'Yes . . . I would like to try.
Nobody asked me before,
but I would like to write a prayer . . .'

Some students were used to praying,
others never prayed.
Some lived with an easy familiarity
in the house of God,
others wondered if the word 'God'
made any sense at all . . .
Some were regular churchgoers,
others never went
or had stopped going because of
boredom or unbelief.
But all wrote a prayer and
wanted others to read it."

Henri Nouwen
Intimacy

REDISCOVERY

Shared prayer with friends
is a new experience
for many people.
For many, also,
it has meant the rediscovery
of meaningful prayer.

Whether the shared prayer
consists in sharing
"peak" or "depth" experiences,
or whether
it focuses on sharing
prayerful reflections on Scripture,
is unimportant.

The important thing is
the sharing.
Jesus said: "Where two or three
come together in my name,
I am there with them."

Matthew 18:20

INSIGHT

For new insight into prayer,
Western man, in recent years,
has begun to turn to other prayer traditions.
One place he has turned
is to the East.

Eastern mysticism
reflects a world view more in harmony with
that of modern physics.
The stress in the East is on totality,
rather than on individuality.

Stemming from its world view,
Eastern philosophy places more value upon
pure consciousness than upon
consciousness of "something".
The prevailing desire is not so much
to know reality as to become it.

Decades of Western rationalism
cry out for the "cool" of intuition.
And intuition is ennobled in Eastern thought,
where paradox flourishes.

In Zen Buddhism, the riddle or *koan* exemplifies
the accent on non-discursive thinking.

Eastern religions are less highly organized.
Disenchantment with established religion
may account for some of the affinity
for a less structured form of worship.

Eastern prayer stresses prolonged
quiet and meditation, whereas Western prayer
tends to be of the "short-order" quality.
One thinks of Buddha's command:
"Don't just do something. Stand there!"

Eastern prayer traditions
pay more realistic attention to the body.
Yoga seems to be the best example of this.
Knowledge of great prayer traditions
can no longer be considered a fad or luxury;
rather, a serious responsibility.

Adapted from
Jane Marie Richardson
"Prayer and Contemporary Man"

PILGRIM'S PROGRESS

To some extent
prayer comes naturally to man.
Like anything innate,
it often tends to follow
a natural rhythm identifiable with growth.

"During childhood
recited prayer predominates . . .
words learned by heart or read from a book . . .

From adolesence to manhood
meditative prayer develops . . .
We also find spoken prayer during this period.
This species, while focusing upon
a subject of one's own choosing,
breaks forth spontaneously . . .
It may be the outburst of an emotion of joy,
praise, gratefulness, sorrow . . .

Finally, silent prayer
is the prayer of the mature man, whose soul
remains speechless in the presence of God,
aware of the inadequacy of whatever it may say,
simply content
to rest in this entrancing company."

Michael Lapierre
"Progress in Prayer"

But this does not mean
that we should always pray in this or that way.
Indeed, at times, for various reasons,
we may find that a particular form of prayer
may or may not be suitable,
because of certain special circumstances
we find ourselves in.

If a certain prayer style helps, why not use it;
If it doesn't, why not discard it for the time being
and try another.

DARE REBIRTH

I am the vine, you are the branches.
Whoever remains in me, and I in him,
will bear much fruit;
for you can do nothing without me . . .
If you remain in me, and my words remain in you,
then you will ask for anything you wish,
and you shall have it . . .

This is my commandment: love one another,
just as I love you.
The greatest love a man can have for his friends
is to give his life for them.
And you are my friends, if you do what I command.
I do not call you servants any longer,
because a servant does not know
what his master is doing.
Instead, I call you friends, because I have told you
everything I heard from my Father.
You did not choose me; I chose you,
and appointed you to go and bear much fruit,
the kind of fruit that endures.

John 15:5-16

NEW HORIZON

Set me adrift in a sea of hope,
And I'll set my sail to a new horizon.

O GLAD, EXULTING, CULMINATING SONG!

A vigor more than earth's is in thy notes . . .
A reborn race appears—a perfect world, all joy!

Women and men in wisdom, innocence and health—all joy!
Riotous laughing bacchanals fill'd with joy!

War, sorrow, suffering gone—
    the rank earth purged—nothing but joy left!

The ocean fill'd with joy—the atmosphere all joy!

Joy! joy in freedom, worship, love!
    joy in the ecstasy of life!

Enough to merely be! enough to breathe!

Joy! joy! all over joy!

Walt Whitman